TO

Jessica

FROM

Harry and Pat Abercrombie

DATE

June 1, 2012

The ROAD AHEAD

Daily Thoughts and Devotions for Your Life

Freeman-Smith, a division of Worthy Media, Inc.
134 Franklin Road, Suite 200, Brentwood, Tennessee 37027

The quoted ideas expressed in this book (but not Scripture verses) are not, in all cases, exact quotations, as some have been edited for clarity and brevity. In all cases, the author has attempted to maintain the speaker's original intent. In some cases, quoted material for this book was obtained from secondary sources, primarily print media. While every effort was made to ensure the accuracy of these sources, the accuracy cannot be guaranteed. For additions, deletions, corrections, or clarifications in future editions of this text, please write Freeman-Smith.

Cover Design by Kim Russell / Wahoo Designs
Page Layout by Bart Dawson

ISBN 978-1-60587-356-5

Printed in the United States of America

The ROAD AHEAD

Daily Thoughts and Devotions for Your Life

INTRODUCTION

As you graduate into your next phase of life, you've got decisions to make . . . lots of them. In fact, you may be facing a multitude of choices: where to live, where to work, or what to do about your personal relationships. These decisions are important, of course, but they pale in comparison to a single overriding choice that will fashion your eternal destiny. That decision is your commitment to form a personal, saving relationship with Jesus Christ.

Daily life is woven together with the threads of habit, and no habit is more important to your spiritual growth than the discipline of daily prayer and devotion to God. On the pages that follow, you'll be asked to spend a few minutes each day thinking about ways that you and God, working together, can organize your life, prioritize your efforts, redirect your thoughts, and follow the path that your heavenly Father intends for you to take. When you do these things, you'll receive the peace and the spiritual abundance that can, and should, be yours. So, for the next 100 days, please try this experiment: Read a chapter a day and internalize the ideas that you find here. If you are not, the simple act of giving God a few minutes each morning will change the tone and direction of your life.

You have worked hard to graduate, and you are about to embark upon a new beginning, the next phase of your journey. If you make every step of that journey with Christ by your side—and if you build your faith upon the firm foundation of God's promises—you will claim for yourself the abundance and grace that God intends for your life. So today, if you do nothing else, accept God's grace with open arms. When you do, you will be the proud recipient of a priceless gift that will change your life forever and endure throughout eternity.

Devotion #1

IT'S A NEW DAY

Then the One seated on the throne said,
"Look! I am making everything new."
Revelation 21:5 HCSB

Welcome to the next stage of your journey. This day, like every other, will contain countless opportunities to serve God, to seek His will, and to obey His teachings. But this day will also offer countless opportunities to stray from God's commandments and to wander far from His path. Your challenge is to seek God's will and to follow His direction on the road ahead.

Sometimes, the road ahead is well-marked; sometimes it's not. But if you become confused or disoriented, you need never stay lost for long. God is always ready, willing, and able to guide your path if you let Him. Your job, simply put, is to let Him.

So, as you make the transition from one phase of life to another, consider this day a new beginning. Consider it a fresh start, a renewed opportunity to serve your Creator with willing hands and a loving heart. Ask God to renew your sense of purpose as He guides your steps. When you ask for His guidance, He will give it. And you will be eternally blessed.

MORE FROM GOD'S WORD ABOUT NEW BEGINNINGS

We must do the works of Him who sent Me while it is day. Night is coming when no one can work.
John 9:4 HCSB

But those who wait on the Lord shall renew their strength; they shall mount up with wings like eagles, they shall run and not be weary, they shall walk and not faint.
Isaiah 40:31 NKJV

Therefore if anyone is in Christ, he is a new creature; the old things passed away; behold, new things have come.
2 Corinthians 5:17 HCSB

You are being renewed in the spirit of your minds; you put on the new man, the one created according to God's likeness in righteousness and purity of the truth.
Ephesians 4:23-24 HCSB

I will give you a new heart and put a new spirit within you.
Ezekiel 36:26 HCSB

No matter what we've been,
when we are touched by God,
we can honestly say,
"Now I'm no longer the same!"
Gloria Gaither

No matter how badly we have failed,
we can always get up and begin again.
Our God is the God of new beginnings.
Warren Wiersbe

God is not running an antique shop!
He is making all things new!
Vance Havner

SOMETHING TO THINK ABOUT

If you're graduating into a new phase of life, be sure to make God your partner. If you do, He'll guide your steps, He'll help carry your burdens, and He'll help you focus on the things that really matter.

Devotion #2

PUT GOD FIRST

You shall have no other gods before Me.
Exodus 20:3 NKJV

Who is in charge of your heart? Is it God, or is it something else? Have you given Christ your heart, your soul, your talents, your time, and your testimony? Or are you giving Him little more than a few hours each Sunday morning?

In the book of Exodus, God warns that we should place no gods before Him. Yet all too often, we place our Lord in second, third, or fourth place as we worship other things. When we unwittingly place possessions or relationships above our love for the Creator, we create big problems for ourselves.

Have you chosen to allow God to rule your heart? Make certain that the honest answer to this question is a resounding yes. In the life of every thoughtful believer, God comes first. And that's precisely the place that He deserves in your heart.

MORE FROM GOD'S WORD ABOUT PUTTING GOD FIRST

Be careful not to forget the Lord.
Deuteronomy 6:12 HCSB

It is good to give thanks to the Lord,
and to sing praises to Your name, O Most High;
to declare Your lovingkindness in the morning,
and Your faithfulness every night.
Psalm 92:1-2 NKJV

Love the Lord your God with all your heart,
with all your soul, and with all your strength.
Deuteronomy 6:5 HCSB

The Devil said to Him, "I will give You their splendor and all this authority, because it has been given over to me, and I can give it to anyone I want. If You, then, will worship me, all will be Yours." And Jesus answered him, "It is written: You shall worship the Lord your God, and Him alone you shall serve."
Luke 4:6-8 HCSB

The Lord bless you and protect you; the Lord make His face shine on you, and be gracious to you.
Numbers 6:24-25 HCSB

One with God is a majority.
Billy Graham

God is the beyond in the midst of our life.
Dietrich Bonhoeffer

You can't get second things by putting them first;
you can get second things only by
putting first things first.
C. S. Lewis

Love has its source in God,
for love is the very essence of His being.
Kay Arthur

SOMETHING TO THINK ABOUT

Today, spend a few minutes thinking about your relationship with God. Is it really an intimate one-on-one connection, or are you allowing other things to come between you and your Creator? Write down three specific steps that you can take right now to forge a stronger bond with your Heavenly Father.

Devotion #3

PAY ATTENTION TO GOD

For where your treasure is, there your heart will be also.
Luke 12:34 HCSB

As you begin the next leg of your life's journey, please remember that God deserves your undivided attention. Are you giving it to Him? Hopefully so.

When you focus your thoughts and prayers on the One from Galilee, you'll start building a better life and better relationships. But beware: the world will try to convince you that "other things" are more important than your faith. These messages are both false and dangerous—don't believe them.

When it comes to your spiritual, emotional, and personal growth, absolutely nothing is more important than your faith. So do yourself and your loved ones a favor: focus on God and His only begotten Son. Your loved ones will be glad you did . . . and so will you.

God is the beyond in the midst of our life.
Dietrich Bonhoeffer

Make a plan now to keep a daily appointment with God. The enemy is going to tell you to set it aside, but you must carve out the time. If you're too busy to meet with the Lord, friend, then you are simply too busy.
Charles Swindoll

Huge as this universe is, God has complete power over it, as you have with a ball which you toss in your hand.
C. H. Spurgeon

SOMETHING TO THINK ABOUT

God is trying to get your attention. Are you listening? Having trouble hearing God? If so, slow yourself down, tune out the distractions, and listen carefully. God has important things to say; your task is to be still and listen.

Devotion #4

GOD HAS BIG PLANS FOR YOU

But as it is written: What no eye has seen and no ear has heard, and what has never come into a man's heart, is what God has prepared for those who love Him.
1 Corinthians 2:9 HCSB

God has plans for your life. Big plans. But He won't force you to follow His will; to the contrary, He has given you free will, the ability to make choices and decisions on your own. With the freedom to choose comes the responsibility of living with the consequences of the choices you make.

The most important decision of your life is, of course, your commitment to accept Jesus Christ as your personal Lord and Savior. And once your eternal destiny is secured, you will undoubtedly ask yourself the question "What now, Lord?" If you earnestly seek God's will for your life, you will find it . . . in time.

Sometimes, God's plans are crystal clear, but other times, He leads us through the wilderness before He delivers us to the Promised Land. So be patient, keep searching, and keep praying. If you do, then in time, God will answer your prayers and make His plans known.

As you begin your life after graduation, study God's Word and be ever-watchful for His signs. Associate with fellow Christians who will encourage your spiritual growth and listen to that inner voice that speaks to you in the quiet moments of your daily devotionals. God is here, and He intends to use you in wonderful, unexpected ways. Listen . . . He is here, even now.

God surrounds you with opportunity. You and I are free in Jesus Christ, not to do whatever we want, but to be all that God wants us to be.

Warren Wiersbe

When the dream of our heart is one that God has planted there, a strange happiness flows into us. At that moment, all of the spiritual resources of the universe are released to help us. Our praying is then at one with the will of God and becomes a channel for the Creator's purposes for us and our world.

Catherine Marshall

SOMETHING TO THINK ABOUT

God has a plan for your life, a definite purpose that you can fulfill . . . or not. Your challenge is to pray for God's guidance and to follow wherever He leads.

Devotion #5

FINDING NEW PURPOSE

I, therefore, the prisoner in the Lord, urge you to walk worthy of the calling you have received.
Ephesians 4:1 HCSB

Now that school is a not-so-distant memory, you may be faced with a multitude of decisions: where to live, where to work, what to do about your personal relationships. And hopefully, you have also decided that graduation is just the beginning, not the end, of your spiritual and intellectual journey.

You may be asking yourself an important question: "What does God want me to do with my life?" It's an easy question to ask but, for many of us, a difficult question to answer. Why? Because God's purposes aren't always clear to us. Sometimes we wander aimlessly in a wilderness of our own making. And sometimes, we struggle mightily against God in a vain effort to find success and happiness through our own means, not His.

How can we know precisely what God's intentions are? The answer, of course, is that even the most well-intentioned believers face periods of uncertainty and doubt about the direction of their lives.

When you arrive at one of life's inevitable crossroads, that is precisely the moment when you should turn your thoughts and prayers toward God. When you do, He will make Himself known to you in a time and manner of His choosing.

Are you earnestly seeking to discern God's purpose for your life? If so, this book is intended to remind you of several important facts: 1. God has a plan for your life; 2. If you seek that plan sincerely and prayerfully, you will find it; 3. When you discover God's purpose for your life, you will experience abundance, peace, joy, and power—God's power. And that's the only kind of power that really matters.

MORE FROM GOD'S WORD ABOUT DISCOVERING YOUR PURPOSE

For it is God who is working among you both the willing and the working for His good purpose.
Philippians 2:13 HCSB

Commit your activities to the Lord and your plans will be achieved.
Proverbs 16:3 HCSB

You reveal the path of life to me; in Your presence is abundant joy; in Your right hand are eternal pleasures.
Psalm 16:11 HCSB

The really committed leave the safety of the harbor, accept the risk of the open seas of faith, and set their compasses for the place of total devotion to God and whatever life adventures He plans for them.

Bill Hybels

God's purposes are often hidden from us.
He owes us no explanations.
We owe Him our complete love and trust.

Warren Wiersbe

In the very place where God has put us, whatever its limitations, whatever kind of work it may be, we may indeed serve the Lord Christ.

Elisabeth Elliot

SOMETHING TO THINK ABOUT

God has a wonderful plan for your life. And the time to start looking for that plan—and living it—is now. (Psalm 16:11)

Devotion #6

THE DECISION TO FOLLOW JESUS

Then He said to them all, "If anyone wants to come with Me, he must deny himself, take up his cross daily, and follow Me."
Luke 9:23 HCSB

With whom will you choose to walk today? Will you walk with shortsighted people who honor the ways of the world, or will you walk with the Son of God? Jesus walks with you. Are you walking with Him? Hopefully, you will choose to walk with Him today and every day of your life.

Jesus has called upon believers of every generation (and that includes you) to follow in His footsteps. And God's Word promises that when you follow in Christ's footsteps, you will learn how to live freely and lightly (Matthew 11:28-30).

Jesus doesn't want you to be a run-of-the-mill, follow-the-crowd kind of person. Jesus wants you to be a "new creation" through Him. And that's exactly what you should want for yourself, too. Nothing is more important than your wholehearted commitment to your Creator and to His only begotten Son. Your faith must never be an afterthought; it must be your ultimate priority, your ultimate possession, and your ultimate passion.

You are the recipient of Christ's love. Accept it enthusiastically and share it passionately. Jesus deserves your extreme enthusiasm; the world deserves it; and you deserve the experience of sharing it.

Will you, with a glad and eager surrender, hand yourself and all that concerns you over into his hands? If you will do this, your soul will begin to know something of the joy of union with Christ.

Hannah Whitall Smith

Our responsibility is to feed from Him, to stay close to Him, to follow Him—because sheep easily go astray—so that we eternally experience the protection and companionship of our Great Shepherd the Lord Jesus Christ.

Franklin Graham

SOMETHING TO THINK ABOUT

If you want to be a little more like Christ, learn about His teachings, follow in His footsteps, and obey His commandments.

Devotion #7

CHOOSING TO BE KIND

Love is patient; love is kind.
1 Corinthians 13:4 HCSB

Kindness is a choice. Sometimes, when we feel happy or generous, we find it easy to be kind. Other times, when we are discouraged or tired, we can scarcely summon the energy to utter a single kind word. But, God's commandment is clear: He intends that we make the conscious choice to treat others with kindness and respect, no matter our circumstances, no matter our emotions.

In the busyness of daily life, it is easy to lose focus, and it is easy to become frustrated. When we are distracted or disappointed, we may neglect to share a kind word or a kind deed. This oversight hurts others, but it hurts us most of all.

Today, be alert for people who need your smile, your kind words, or your helping hand. Make kindness a centerpiece of your dealings with others. They will be blessed, and you will be too.

A little kindly advice is better
than a great deal of scolding.
Fanny Crosby

When you extend hospitality to others,
you're not trying to impress people,
you're trying to reflect God to them.
Max Lucado

When you launch an act of kindness out
into the crosswinds of life,
it will blow kindness back to you.
Dennis Swanberg

Do all the good you can. By all the means you can.
In all the ways you can. In all the places you can.
At all the times you can. To all the people you can.
As long as ever you can.
John Wesley

SOMETHING TO THINK ABOUT

When you make the decision to be a genuinely kind person, you'll make decisions that improve your own life and the lives of your family and friends.

Devotion #8

ON THE ROAD AHEAD, USE YOUR TALENTS

I remind you to keep ablaze the gift of God that is in you.
2 Timothy 1:6 HCSB

Face facts: you have an array of talents that need to be refined. All people possess special gifts—bestowed from the Father above—and you are no exception. But, your particular gift is no guarantee of success; it must be cultivated—by you—or it will go unused . . . and God's gift to you will be squandered.

Are you willing to do the hard work that's required to discover your talents and to develop them? If you are wise, you'll answer "yes." After all, if you don't make the most of your talents, who has the most to lose? You do!

So make a promise to yourself that you will earnestly seek to discover the talents that God has given you. Then, nourish those talents and make them grow. Finally, vow to share your gifts with the world for as long as God gives you the power to do so. After all, the best way to say "Thank You" for God's gifts is to use them.

MORE FROM GOD'S WORD ABOUT USING YOUR TALENTS

According to the grace given to us, we have different gifts: If prophecy, use it according to the standard of faith; if service, in service; if teaching, in teaching; if exhorting, in exhortation; giving, with generosity; leading, with diligence; showing mercy, with cheerfulness.

Romans 12:6-8 HCSB

His master said to him, "Well done, good and faithful slave! You were faithful over a few things; I will put you in charge of many things. Enter your master's joy!"

Matthew 25:21 HCSB

Every good gift and every perfect gift is from above, and cometh down from the Father of lights.

James 1:17 KJV

Do not neglect the gift that is in you.

1 Timothy 4:14 HCSB

Each one has his own gift from God, one in this manner and another in that.

1 Corinthians 7:7 NKJV

Not everyone possesses boundless energy
or a conspicuous talent. We are not equally blessed
with great intellect or physical beauty or emotional
strength. But we have all been given
the same ability to be faithful.

Gigi Graham Tchividjian

You are a unique blend of talents, skills,
and gifts, which makes you an indispensable
member of the body of Christ.

Charles Stanley

You are the only person on earth
who can use your ability.

Zig Ziglar

SOMETHING TO THINK ABOUT

God has given you a unique array of talents and opportunities. If you use your gifts wisely, they're multiplied. If you misuse your gifts—or ignore them altogether—they are lost. God is anxious for you to use your gifts . . . are you?

Devotion #9

STUDYING GOD'S WORD

All Scripture is given by inspiration of God, and is profitable for doctrine, for reproof, for correction, for instruction in righteousness, that the man of God may be complete, thoroughly equipped for every good work.
2 Timothy 3:16-17 NKJV

Now that you've graduated, you can put your books aside . . . except for The Book: God's Holy Word. The Bible is a roadmap for life here on earth and for life eternal; it should be the map for you.

As believers, we must study the Bible daily and meditate upon its meaning for our lives. Otherwise, we deprive ourselves of a priceless gift from our Creator. God's Holy Word is, indeed, a transforming, life-changing, one-of-a-kind treasure. A passing acquaintance with the Good Book is insufficient for Christians who seek to obey God's Word and to understand His will.

Jonathan Edwards advised, "Be assiduous in reading the Holy Scriptures. This is the fountain whence all knowledge in divinity must be derived. Therefore let not this treasure lie by you neglected."

God's Holy Word is, indeed, a priceless, one-of-a-kind treasure. Handle it with care, but more importantly, handle it every day.

Study the Bible and observe how the persons
behaved and how God dealt with them.
There is explicit teaching on every condition of life.
Corrie ten Boom

Nobody ever outgrows Scripture;
the book widens and deepens with our years.
C. H. Spurgeon

I study the Bible as I gather apples.
First, I shake the whole tree that the ripest
might fall. Then I shake each limb;
I shake each branch and every twig.
Then, I look under every leaf.
Martin Luther

SOMETHING TO THINK ABOUT

It's up to you: Nobody can study the Bible for you; you've got to study it for yourself. And that's exactly what you should do.

Devotion #10

AVOIDING THE TEMPTATIONS

Put on the whole armor of God,
that you may be able to stand
against the wiles of the devil.
Ephesians 6:11 NKJV

You live a temptation-filled world. The devil is hard at work in your neighborhood, and so are his helpers. Here in the 21st century, the bad guys are working around the clock to lead you astray. That's why you must remain vigilant.

In a letter to believers, Peter offers a stern warning: "Your adversary, the devil, prowls around like a roaring lion, seeking someone to devour" (1 Peter 5:8 NASB). What was true in New Testament times is equally true in our own. Satan tempts his prey and then devours them (and it's up to you—and only you—to make sure that you're not one of the ones being devoured!).

As a believer who seeks a radical relationship with Jesus, you must beware because temptations are everywhere. Satan is determined to win; you must be equally determined that he does not.

The Lord knows how to deliver
the godly out of temptations.
2 Peter 2:9 NKJV

Jesus faced every temptation known to humanity
so that He could identify with us.
Beth Moore

Our battles are first won or lost in the secret places
of our will in God's presence,
never in full view of the world.
Oswald Chambers

Flee temptation without leaving
a forwarding address.
Barbara Johnson

SOMETHING TO THINK ABOUT

If life's inevitable temptations seem to be getting the best of you, try praying more often, even if many of those prayers are simply brief, "open-eyed" requests to your Father in heaven.

Devotion #11

WHEN YOU MAKE A MISTAKE

The one who conceals his sins will not prosper,
but whoever confesses and renounces them
will find mercy.
Proverbs 28:13 HCSB

We are imperfect beings living in an imperfect world; mistakes are simply part of the price we pay for being here. Yet, even though mistakes are an inevitable part of life's journey, repeated mistakes should not be. When we commit the inevitable blunders of life, we must correct them, learn from them, and pray for the wisdom to avoid those same mistakes in the future. If we are successful, our missteps become lessons, and our lives become adventures in growth.

Mistakes are the price we pay for being human; repeated mistakes are the price we pay for being stubborn. But, if we are wise enough to learn from our experiences, we continue to mature throughout every stage of life. And that's precisely what God intends for us to do.

*God, create a clean heart for me
and renew a steadfast spirit within me.*
Psalm 51:10 HCSB

Father, take our mistakes and turn them
into opportunities.
Max Lucado

I hope you don't mind me telling you all this.
One can learn only by seeing one's mistakes.
C. S. Lewis

God is able to take mistakes,
when they are committed to Him,
and make of them something
for our good and for His glory.
Ruth Bell Graham

SOMETHING TO THINK ABOUT

When you make mistakes (and you will) the best time to fix those mistakes is now, not later.

Devotion #12

FOLLOW YOUR CONSCIENCE

For indeed, the kingdom of God is within you.
Luke 17:21 NKJV

God gave you a conscience for a very good reason: to make your path conform to His will. Billy Graham correctly observed, "Most of us follow our conscience as we follow a wheelbarrow. We push it in front of us in the direction we want to go." To do so, of course, is a profound mistake. Yet all of us, on occasion, have failed to listen to the voice that God planted in our hearts, and all of us have suffered the consequences.

Wise believers make it a practice to listen carefully to that quiet internal voice. Count yourself among that number. When your conscience speaks, listen and learn. In all likelihood, God is trying to get His message through. And in all likelihood, it is a message that you desperately need to hear.

Now the goal of our instruction is love from a pure heart, a good conscience, and a sincere faith.
1 Timothy 1:5 HCSB

The integrity of the upright will guide them.
Proverbs 11:3 NKJV

The convicting work of the Holy Spirit awakens, disturbs, and judges.
Franklin Graham

Every secret act of character, conviction, and courage has been observed in living color by our omniscient God.
Bill Hybels

A good conscience is a continual feast.
Francis Bacon

SOMETHING TO THINK ABOUT

If your friends are telling you one thing and your conscience is telling you something else, trust your conscience.

Devotion #13

WISE CHOICES 101

Therefore, everyone who hears these words of Mine and acts on them will be like a sensible man who built his house on the rock. The rain fell, the rivers rose, and the winds blew and pounded that house. Yet it didn't collapse, because its foundation was on the rock.

Matthew 7:24–25 HCSB

Sometimes, amid the concerns of everyday life, we lose perspective. Life seems out of balance as we confront an array of demands that sap our strength and cloud our thoughts. What's needed is a renewed faith, a fresh perspective, and God's wisdom.

Here in the 21st century, commentary is commonplace and information is everywhere. But the ultimate source of wisdom, the kind of timeless wisdom that God willingly shares with His children, is still available from a single unique source: the Holy Bible.

The wisdom of the world changes with the ever-shifting sands of public opinion. God's wisdom does not. His wisdom is eternal. It never changes. And it most certainly is the wisdom that you must use to plan your day, your life, and your eternal destiny.

MORE FROM GOD'S WORD ABOUT DISCOVERING WISDOM

But from Him you are in Christ Jesus, who for us became wisdom from God, as well as righteousness, sanctification, and redemption.

1 Corinthians 1:30 HCSB

For God has not given us a spirit of fearfulness, but one of power, love, and sound judgment.

2 Timothy 1:7 HCSB

Now if any of you lacks wisdom, he should ask God, who gives to all generously and without criticizing, and it will be given to him.

James 1:5 HCSB

But the wisdom from above is first pure, then peace-loving, gentle, compliant, full of mercy and good fruits, without favoritism and hypocrisy.

James 3:17 HCSB

Wisdom is the principal thing; therefore get wisdom. And in all your getting, get understanding.

Proverbs 4:7 NKJV

Don't expect wisdom to come into your life like great chunks of rock on a conveyor belt. Wisdom comes privately from God as a by-product of right decisions, godly reactions, and the application of spiritual principles to daily circumstances.

Charles Swindoll

Wisdom is the right use of knowledge. To know is not to be wise. Many men know a great deal, and are all the greater fools for it. But to know how to use knowledge is to have wisdom.

C. H. Spurgeon

If we neglect the Bible, we cannot expect to benefit from the wisdom and direction that result from knowing God's Word.

Vonette Bright

SOMETHING TO THINK ABOUT

If you own a Bible, you have ready access to God's wisdom. Your job is to read, to understand, and to apply His teachings to your life . . . starting now and ending never.

Devotion #14

WALKING IN THE LIGHT

Then Jesus spoke to them again:
"I am the light of the world. Anyone who follows Me will never walk in the darkness, but will have the light of life."
John 8:12 HCSB

God's Holy Word instructs us that Jesus is, "the way, the truth, and the life" (John 14:6-7). Without Christ, we are as far removed from salvation as the east is removed from the west. And without Christ, we can never know the ultimate truth: God's truth.

Truth is God's way: He commands that His believers live in truth, and He rewards those who do so. Jesus is the personification of God's liberating truth, a truth that offers salvation to mankind.

Do you seek to walk with God? Do you seek to feel His presence and His peace? Then you must walk in truth; you must walk in the light; you must walk with the Savior. There is simply no other way.

I am the door. If anyone enters by Me, he will be saved.
John 10:9 NKJV

Image is what people think we are;
integrity is what we really are.
John Maxwell

Victory is the result of Christ's life lived out in the believer. It is important to see that victory, not defeat, is God's purpose for His children.
Corrie ten Boom

Jesus differs from all other teachers; they reach the ear, but he instructs the heart; they deal with the outward letter, but he imparts an inward taste for the truth.
C. H. Spurgeon

SOMETHING TO THINK ABOUT

God says that if you seek, you will find. So seek God, and He will reveal His will and His way.

Devotion #15

MEET WITH GOD EVERY MORNING

He awakens [Me] each morning;
He awakens My ear to listen like those being instructed.
The Lord God has opened My ear,
and I was not rebellious; I did not turn back.
Isaiah 50:4-5 HCSB

Each new day is a gift from God, and if we are wise, we spend a few quiet moments each morning thanking the Giver. Daily life is woven together with the threads of habit, and no habit is more important to our spiritual health than the discipline of daily prayer and devotion to the Creator.

When we begin each day with heads bowed and hearts lifted, we remind ourselves of God's love, His protection, and His commandments. And if we are wise, we align our priorities for the coming day with the teachings and commandments that God has given us through His Holy Word.

Are you seeking to change some aspect of your life? Do you seek to improve the condition of your spiritual or physical health? If so, ask for God's help and ask for it many times each day . . . starting with your morning devotional.

I will instruct you and show you the way to go;
with My eye on you, I will give counsel.
Psalm 32:8 HCSB

A person with no devotional life generally struggles
with faith and obedience.
Charles Stanley

Maintenance of the devotional mood is
indispensable to success in the Christian life.
A. W. Tozer

I suggest you discipline yourself to spend time daily
in a systematic reading of God's Word.
Make this "quiet time" a priority
that nobody can change.
Warren Wiersbe

SOMETHING TO THINK ABOUT

Get reacquainted with God every day: Would you like a foolproof formula for a better relationship with your Creator? Then stay in close contact with Him.

Devotion #16

YOUR BIG OPPORTUNITIES

Therefore, as we have opportunity, we must work for the good of all, especially for those who belong to the household of faith.
Galatians 6:10 HCSB

Are you excited about the opportunities of today and thrilled by the possibilities of tomorrow? Do you confidently expect God to lead you to a place of abundance, peace, and joy? And, when your days on earth are over, do you expect to receive the priceless gift of eternal life? If you trust God's promises, and if you have welcomed God's Son into your heart, then you believe that your future is intensely and eternally bright.

Today, as you prepare to meet the duties of everyday life, pause and consider God's promises. And then think for a moment about the wonderful future that awaits all believers, including you. God has promised that your future is secure. Trust that promise, and celebrate the life of abundance and eternal joy that is now yours through Christ.

I am able to do all things through Him
who strengthens me.
Philippians 4:13 HCSB

God surrounds you with opportunity.
You and I are free in Jesus Christ,
not to do whatever we want,
but to be all that God wants us to be.
Warren Wiersbe

Great opportunities often disguise themselves
in small tasks.
Rick Warren

A wise man makes more opportunities
than he finds.
Francis Bacon

SOMETHING TO THINK ABOUT

God gives you opportunities for a reason . . . to use them. Billy Graham observed, "Life is a glorious opportunity." That's sound advice, so keep looking for your opportunities until you find them, and when you find them, take advantage of them sooner rather than later.

Devotion #17

STAY INVOLVED IN YOUR CHURCH

For we are God's fellow workers; you are God's field, you are God's building.
1 Corinthians 3:9 NKJV

The Bible teaches that we should worship God in our hearts and in our churches (Acts 20:28). We have clear instructions to "feed the church of God" and to worship our Creator in the presence of fellow believers.

We live in a world that is teeming with temptations and distractions—a world where good and evil struggle in a constant battle to win our minds, our hearts, and our souls. Our challenge, of course, is to ensure that we cast our lot on the side of God. One way that we remain faithful to Him is through the practice of regular, purposeful worship. When we worship the Father faithfully and fervently, we are blessed.

The church belongs to God; it is His just as certainly as we are His. When we help build God's church, we bear witness to the changes that He has made in our lives.

Are you an active member of your own fellowship? Are you a builder of bridges inside the four walls of your church and outside it? Do you contribute to God's glory by contributing your time and your talents to a close-knit band of believers? Hopefully so. The fellowship of believers is intended to be a powerful tool for spreading God's Good News and uplifting His children. And God intends for you to be a fully contributing member of that fellowship. Your intentions should be the same.

The Bible knows nothing of solitary religion.
John Wesley

How beautiful it is to learn that grace isn't fragile,
and that in the family of God
we can fail and not be a failure.
Gloria Gaither

It has always been the work of the church to bring
others to belief in Christ and to experience
a personal relationship with Him.
Charles Stanley

SOMETHING TO THINK ABOUT

Make church a celebration, not an obligation: Your attitude towards church is important, in part, because it is contagious . . . so celebrate accordingly!

Devotion #18

THE POWER OF PERSEVERANCE

Therefore, my dear brothers, be steadfast, immovable, always abounding in the Lord's work, knowing that your labor in the Lord is not in vain.
1 Corinthians 15:58 HCSB

Now that you've graduated, the hard work is over . . . right? Wrong! Even if you have worked very hard in school, there is still more work to do . . . much more work. In fact, the most challenging years of your life are probably still ahead, so prepare yourself. And learn to be patient.

Our Savior, Christ Jesus, finished what He began. Despite the torture He endured, despite the shame of the cross, Jesus was steadfast in His faithfulness to God. We, too, must remain faithful, especially during times of hardship and pain.

Perhaps you are in a hurry for God to reveal His plans for your life. If so, be forewarned: God operates on His own timetable, not yours. Sometimes, God may answer your prayers with silence, and when He does, you must patiently persevere. In times of trouble, seek God through prayer and lean upon His strength. Whatever your problem, He can handle it. Your job is to keep persevering until He does.

MORE FROM GOD'S WORD ABOUT PERSEVERANCE

Do you not know that the runners in a stadium all race, but only one receives the prize? Run in such a way that you may win. Now everyone who competes exercises self-control in everything. However, they do it to receive a perishable crown, but we an imperishable one.

1 Corinthians 9:24-25 HCSB

But as for you, be strong; don't be discouraged, for your work has a reward.

2 Chronicles 15:7 HCSB

I have fought the good fight, I have finished the race, I have kept the faith.

2 Timothy 4:7 HCSB

So we must not get tired of doing good, for we will reap at the proper time if we don't give up.

Galatians 6:9 HCSB

Let us lay aside every weight and the sin that so easily ensnares us, and run with endurance the race that lies before us, keeping our eyes on Jesus, the source and perfecter of our faith.

Hebrews 12:1-2 HCSB

Only the man who follows the command of Jesus single-mindedly and unresistingly lets his yoke rest upon him, finds his burden easy, and under its gentle pressure receives the power to persevere in the right way.

Dietrich Bonhoeffer

In all negotiations of difficulties, a man may not look to sow and reap at once. He must prepare his business and so ripen it by degrees.

Francis Bacon

I learned as never before that persistent calling upon the Lord breaks through every stronghold of the devil, for nothing is impossible with God. For Christians in these troubled times, there is simply no other way.

Jim Cymbala

SOMETHING TO THINK ABOUT

Are you being tested? Call upon God. God can give you the strength to persevere, and that's exactly what you should ask Him to do.

Devotion #19

TALK THINGS OVER WITH GOD

If you don't know what you're doing,
pray to the Father. He loves to help. You'll get his help,
and won't be condescended to when you ask for it.
Ask boldly, believingly, without a second thought.
People who "worry their prayers" are like
wind-whipped waves. Don't think you're going to
get anything from the Master that way, adrift at sea,
keeping all your options open.
James 1:5-8 MSG

Are you faced with a difficult choice or an important decision? Then pray about it. If you talk to God sincerely and often, He won't lead you astray. Instead, God will guide you and help you make more intelligent choices . . . if you take the time to talk with Him.

If you have questions about whether you should do something or not, pray about it. If there is something you're worried about, ask God to comfort you. If you're having trouble with your relationships, ask God to help you sort things out. As you pray more, you'll discover that God is always near and that He's always ready to hear from you. So don't worry about things; pray about them. God is waiting . . . and listening!

Ask, and it shall be given you; seek, and ye shall find; knock, and it shall be opened unto you: for every one that asketh receiveth; and he that seeketh findeth; and to him that knocketh it shall be opened.

Matthew 7:7-8 KJV

Avail yourself of the greatest privilege this side of heaven: prayer. Jesus Christ died to make this communion and communication with the Father possible.

Billy Graham

Prayer is the same as the breathing of air for the lungs. Exhaling makes us get rid of our dirty air. Inhaling gives clean air. To exhale is to confess, to inhale is to be filled with the Holy Spirit.

Corrie ten Boom

Prayer accomplishes more than anything else.

Bill Bright

SOMETHING TO THINK ABOUT

There's no corner of your life that's too unimportant to pray about, so pray about everything.

Devotion #20

ON THE ROAD AHEAD, LEARN TO MANAGE YOUR TIME WISELY

So teach us to number our days,
that we may gain a heart of wisdom.
Psalm 90:12 NKJV

Time is a nonrenewable gift from God. But sometimes, we treat our time here on earth as if it were not a gift at all: We may be tempted to invest our lives in trivial pursuits and mindless diversions. But our Father in heaven wants us to do more . . . much more.

Are you one of those people who puts things off until the last minute? Do you waste time doing things that don't matter very much while putting off the important things until it's too late to do the job right? If so, it's now time to start making better choices.

It may seem like you've got all the time in the world to do the things you need to do, but time is shorter than you think. Time here on earth is limited . . . use it or lose it!

When you make a vow to God, don't delay fulfilling it,
because He does not delight in fools.
Fulfill what you vow.
Ecclesiastes 5:4 HCSB

To choose time is to save time.
Francis Bacon

The more time you give to something,
the more you reveal its importance
and value to you.
Rick Warren

Frustration is not the will of God.
There is time to do anything and
everything that God wants us to do.
Elisabeth Elliot

SOMETHING TO THINK ABOUT

Every day, you get to choose how you will spend your time. If you choose wisely, you'll improve yourself and your life.

Devotion #21

SPIRITUAL GROWTH DAY BY DAY

When I was a child, I spoke like a child,
I thought like a child, I reasoned like a child.
When I became a man, I put aside childish things.
1 Corinthians 13:11 HCSB

Graduation is an important milestone in your education, but the end of the school year should not mark the end of your intellectual growth. Hopefully, you will keep learning every day that you live. And so it is with spiritual growth: the journey toward spiritual maturity should last a lifetime. As Christians, we can and should continue to grow in the love and the knowledge of our Savior as long as we live.

Norman Vincent Peale had simple advice for believers of all ages. Dr. Peale said, "Ask the God who made you to keep remaking you." That advice, of course, is perfectly sound, but too often ignored.

When we cease to grow, either emotionally or spiritually, we do ourselves and our families a profound disservice. But, if we study God's Word, if we obey His commandments, and if we live in the center of His will, we will not be "stagnant" believers; we will, instead, be growing Christians . . . and that's exactly what God wants for our lives.

In those quiet moments when we open our hearts to God, the Creator who made us keeps remaking us. He gives us direction, perspective, wisdom, and courage. And, the appropriate moment to accept His spiritual gifts is always this one.

For this reason also, since the day we heard this, we haven't stopped praying for you. We are asking that you may be filled with the knowledge of His will in all wisdom and spiritual understanding.

Colossians 1:9 HCSB

I want their hearts to be encouraged and joined together in love, so that they may have all the riches of assured understanding, and have the knowledge of God's mystery—Christ.

Colossians 2:2 HCSB

We look at our burdens and heavy loads, and we shrink from them. But, if we lift them and bind them about our hearts, they become wings, and on them we can rise and soar toward God.

Mrs. Charles E. Cowman

You are either becoming more like Christ every day or you're becoming less like Him. There is no neutral position in the Lord.

Stormie Omartian

When it comes to walking with God, there is no such thing as instant maturity. God doesn't mass produce His saints. He hand tools each one, and it always takes longer than we expected.

Charles Swindoll

I'm not what I want to be.
I'm not what I'm going to be.
But, thank God, I'm not what I was!

Gloria Gaither

Being a Christian means accepting the terms of creation, accepting God as our maker and redeemer, and growing day by day into an increasingly glorious creature in Christ, developing joy, experiencing love, maturing in peace.

Eugene Peterson

If all struggles and sufferings were eliminated, the spirit would no more reach maturity than would the child.

Elisabeth Elliot

SOMETHING TO THINK ABOUT

Growing to spiritual maturity requires a plan. What is yours?

Devotion #22

CHOOSING TO SERVE

If they serve Him obediently,
they will end their days in prosperity
and their years in happiness.
Job 36:11 HCSB

You are a wondrous creation treasured by God . . . how will you respond? Will you consider each day a glorious opportunity to celebrate life and improve your little corner of the world? Hopefully so because your corner of the world, like so many other corners of the world, can use all the help it can get.

Nicole Johnson observed, "We only live once, and if we do it well, once is enough." Her words apply to you. You can make a difference, a big difference in the quality of your own life and the lives of your neighbors, your family, and your friends.

You make the world a better place whenever you find a need and fill it. And in these difficult days, the needs are great—but so are your abilities to meet those needs.

Well done, good and faithful servant; you were faithful over a few things, I will make you ruler over many things. Enter into the joy of your lord.

Matthew 25:21 NKJV

Service is the pathway to real significance.

Rick Warren

Doing something positive toward another person is a practical approach to feeling good about yourself.

Barbara Johnson

Through our service to others, God wants to influence our world for Him.

Vonette Bright

SOMETHING TO THINK ABOUT

Whatever your age, whatever your circumstances, you can serve: Each stage of life's journey is a glorious opportunity to place yourself in the service of the One who is the Giver of all blessings. As long as you live, you should honor God with your service to others.

Devotion #23

BEING A GOOD EXAMPLE

You should be an example to the believers in speech, in conduct, in love, in faith, in purity.
1 Timothy 4:12 HCSB

How do people know that you're a Christian? Well, you can tell them, of course. And make no mistake about it: talking about your faith in God is a very good thing to do. But simply telling people about Jesus isn't enough. You must also be willing to show people how an extremely devoted Christian (like you) should behave.

Is your life a picture book of your creed? Do your actions line up with your beliefs? Are you willing to practice the philosophy that you preach? If so, congratulations. If not, it's time for a change.

Like it or not, your behavior is a powerful example to others. The question is not whether you will be an example to your family and friends; the question is what kind of example will you be.

Corrie ten Boom advised, "Don't worry about what you do not understand. Worry about what you do understand in the Bible but do not live by." And that's sound advice because your family and friends are always watching . . . and so is God.

*Set an example of good works yourself,
with integrity and dignity in your teaching.*
Titus 2:7 HCSB

Among the most joyful people I have known
have been some who seem to have had
no human reason for joy. The sweet fragrance of
Christ has shown through their lives.
Elisabeth Elliot

We must mirror God's love in the midst of a world
full of hatred. We are the mirrors of God's love,
so we may show Jesus by our lives.
Corrie ten Boom

Our walk counts far more than our talk, always!
George Mueller

SOMETHING TO THINK ABOUT

You can choose to be a good example . . . or not. The choice you make will have a big impact on your own life and on the lives of others, so choose carefully.

Devotion #24

THE POWER OF SELF-CONTROL

For this very reason, make every effort
to supplement your faith with goodness,
goodness with knowledge, knowledge with self-control,
self-control with endurance, endurance with godliness.
2 Peter 1:5-6 HCSB

Would you like a winning formula for making smart choices? Think about things first and do things next, not vice versa.

Are you, at times, just a little bit too impulsive? Do you react first and think about your reaction second? If so, God wants to have a little chat with you.

God's Word is clear: as a believer, you are called to lead a life of discipline, diligence, moderation, and maturity. But the world often tempts you to behave otherwise. Everywhere you turn, or so it seems, you are encouraged to give in to any number of powerful temptations. So you should plan on being tempted . . . and you should plan on being ready to say, "No!"

The effective Christians of history have been men and women of great personal discipline—mental discipline, discipline of the body, discipline of the tongue, and discipline of the emotion.

Billy Graham

Your thoughts are the determining factor as to whose mold you are conformed to. Control your thoughts and you control the direction of your life.

Charles Stanley

Love, joy, peace, patience, kindness, goodness, faithfulness, gentleness, and self-control.
To these I commit my day. If I succeed, I will give thanks. If I fail, I will seek his grace.
And then, when this day is done,
I will place my head on my pillow and rest.

Max Lucado

SOMETHING TO THINK ABOUT

If you're just a little bit too impulsive, you'll make unwise choices. So when in doubt, slow down, think, and pray before you act.

Devotion #25

BEYOND SELF-CRITICISM

For it was You who created my inward parts;
You knit me together in my mother's womb.
I will praise You, because I have been remarkably and wonderfully made.
Psalm 139:13-14 HCSB

When you feel better about yourself, you make better choices. But sometimes, it's hard to feel good about yourself, especially when you live in a society that keeps sending out the message that you've got to be perfect.

Are you your own worst critic? And in response to that criticism, are you constantly trying to transform yourself into a person who meets society's expectations, but not God's expectations? If so, it's time to become a little more understanding of the person you see whenever you look into the mirror.

Millions of words have been written about various ways to improve self-esteem. Yet, maintaining a healthy self-image is, to a surprising extent, a matter of doing three things: 1. Obeying God 2. Thinking healthy thoughts 3. Finding things to do that please your Creator and yourself. When you concentrate on these things, your self-image will tend to take care of itself.

For You have made him a little lower than the angels,
And You have crowned him with glory and honor.
Psalm 8:5 NKJV

Find satisfaction in him who made you,
and only then find satisfaction in yourself
as part of his creation.
St. Augustine

The meek man is not a human mouse afflicted with a sense of his own inferiority. Rather he may be in his moral life as bold as a lion and as strong as Samson; but he has stopped being fooled about himself. He has accepted God's estimate of his own life. He knows he is as weak and helpless as God declared him to be, but paradoxically, he knows at the same time that he is in the sight of God of more importance than angels. In himself, nothing; in God, everything. That is his motto.
A. W. Tozer

SOMETHING TO THINK ABOUT

You don't have to be perfect to follow in Christ's footsteps. Jesus doesn't expect your perfection—He expects your participation.

Devotion #26

FORGIVENESS NOW

All bitterness, anger and wrath, insult and slander must be removed from you, along with all wickedness. And be kind and compassionate to one another, forgiving one another, just as God also forgave you in Christ.
Ephesians 4:31-32 HCSB

Are you the kind of person who has a tough time forgiving and forgetting? If so, welcome to the club. Most of us find it difficult to forgive the people who have hurt us. And that's too bad because life would be much simpler if we could forgive people "once and for all" and be done with it. Yet forgiveness is seldom that easy. Usually, the decision to forgive is straightforward, but the process of forgiving is more difficult. Forgiveness is a journey that requires effort, time, perseverance, and prayer.

If there exists even one person whom you have not forgiven (and that includes yourself), obey God's commandment: forgive that person today. And remember that bitterness, anger, and regret are not part of God's plan for your life. Forgiveness is.

If you sincerely wish to forgive someone, pray for that person. And then pray for yourself by asking God to heal your heart. Don't expect forgiveness to be easy or quick, but rest assured: with God as your partner, you can forgive . . . and you will.

And whenever you stand praying, if you have anything against anyone, forgive him, so that your Father in heaven may also forgive you your wrongdoing.
Mark 11:25 HCSB

We cannot out-sin God's ability to forgive us.
Beth Moore

We are products of our past,
but we don't have to be prisoners of it.
God specializes in giving people a fresh start.
Rick Warren

Our Lord worked with people as they were,
and He was patient—not tolerant of sin,
but compassionate.
Vance Havner

SOMETHING TO THINK ABOUT

Holding a grudge? Drop it. Never expect other people to be more forgiving than you are. And remember: the best time to forgive is now.

Devotion #27

DOING WHAT'S RIGHT

But seek first the kingdom of God and His righteousness, and all these things will be provided for you.
Matthew 6:33 HCSB

Oswald Chambers, the author of the Christian classic devotional text *My Utmost for His Highest,* advised, "Never support an experience which does not have God as its source, and faith in God as its result." These words serve as a powerful reminder that, as Christians, we are called to walk with God and obey His commandments. But, we live in a world that presents us with countless temptations to stray far from God's path. We Christians, when confronted with sin, have clear instructions: Walk—or better yet run—in the opposite direction.

When we seek righteousness in our own lives—and when we seek the companionship of those who do likewise—we reap the spiritual rewards that God intends for our lives. When we live righteously and according to God's commandments, He blesses us in ways that we cannot fully understand.

Today, as you consider the exciting possibilities of life after graduation, make yourself this promise: Support only those activities that further God's kingdom and your own spiritual growth. Be an example of righteous living to your friends, to your neighbors, and to your family. Then, prepare to reap the blessings that God has promised to all those who live according to His will and His Word.

Christianity says we were created by
a righteous God to flourish and be exhilarated in
a righteous environment. God has "wired" us
in such a way that the more righteous we are,
the more we'll actually enjoy life.

Bill Hybels

Holiness has never been the driving force of
the majority. It is, however, mandatory for anyone
who wants to enter the kingdom.

Elisabeth Elliot

SOMETHING TO THINK ABOUT

If you're not sure what to do . . . slow down and listen to your conscience. That little voice inside your head is remarkably dependable, but you can't depend upon it if you never listen to it. So stop, listen, and learn—your conscience is almost always right.

Devotion #28

BEYOND ANGER

When you are angry, do not sin,
and be sure to stop being angry
before the end of the day.
Do not give the devil a way to defeat you.
Ephesians 4:26–27 NCV

The frustrations of everyday living can sometimes get the better of us, and we allow minor disappointments to cause us major problems. When we allow ourselves to become overly irritated by the inevitable ups and downs of life, we become overstressed, overheated, overanxious, and just plain angry.

As the old saying goes, "Anger usually improves nothing but the arch of a cat's back." So don't allow feelings of anger or frustration to rule your life, or, for that matter, your day—your life is simply too short for that, and you deserve much better treatment than that . . . from yourself.

Don't let your spirit rush to be angry,
for anger abides in the heart of fools.
Ecclesiastes 7:9 HCSB

When you strike out in anger,
you may miss the other person,
but you will always hit yourself.
Jim Gallery

Life is too short to spend it being
angry, bored, or dull.
Barbara Johnson

Anger unresolved will only bring you woe.
Kay Arthur

SOMETHING TO THINK ABOUT

Cool off before you spout off: If you're too angry to have a conversation that is both loving and constructive, put things on hold until you simmer down.

Devotion #29

ON THE ROAD AHEAD, AVOID THE TRAP OF MATERIALISM

And He told them, "Watch out and be on guard against all greed, because one's life is not in the abundance of his possessions."
Luke 12:15 HCSB

Are you overly concerned with the things that money can buy? If so, here's a word of warning: your love for material possessions is getting in the way of your relationship with God.

Up on the stage of life, material possessions should play a rather small role. Of course, we all need the basic necessities like food, clothing, and a place to live. But once we've met those needs, the piling up of possessions creates more problems than it solves. Our real riches, of course, are not of this world. We're never really rich until we are rich in spirit.

Our society is in love with money and the things that money can buy. God is not. God cares about people, not possessions, and so must we. We must, to the best of our abilities, love our neighbors as ourselves, and we must, to the best of our abilities, resist the mighty temptation to place possessions ahead of people.

Money, in and of itself, is not evil; worshipping money is. So today, as you seek better ways to know your Creator, remember that God is almighty, but the dollar is not.

Anyone trusting in his riches will fall,
but the righteous will flourish like foliage.
Proverbs 11:28 HCSB

Greed is enslaving. The more you have,
the more you want—until eventually
avarice consumes you.
Kay Arthur

As faithful stewards of what we have,
ought we not to give earnest thought
to our staggering surplus?
Elisabeth Elliot

SOMETHING TO THINK ABOUT

The world wants you to believe that "money and stuff" can buy happiness. Don't believe it! Genuine happiness comes not from money, but from the things that money can't buy—starting, of course, with your relationship to God and His only begotten Son.

Devotion #30

THE CHOICE TO PAY ATTENTION

Pay careful attention, then,
to how you walk—
not as unwise people but as wise.
Ephesians 5:15 HCSB

You've graduated, but you still have plenty of things to learn. And you can learn a lot about life by paying careful attention to the things that happen around you.

God is trying to teach you things, and you can learn those things the easy way (by paying attention and obeying God's rules) or the hard way (by making the same mistakes over and over again until you finally learn something from them). Of course, it's better to learn things sooner rather than later . . . starting now.

The wise man gives proper appreciation in his life
to his past. He learns to sift the sawdust of heritage
in order to find the nuggets that make
the current moment have any meaning.

Grady Nutt

The only power the devil has is in getting people to
believe his lies. If they don't believe his lies,
he is powerless to get his work done.

Stormie Omartian

Temptation always carries with it some bait
that appeals to our natural desires.
The bait not only attracts us, but it also hides
the fact that yielding to the desire will eventually
bring sorrow and punishment.

Warren Wiersbe

SOMETHING TO THINK ABOUT

You don't have to make every mistake yourself; you can learn from other people's mistakes—and you should. By keeping your eyes and mind open, you can learn some of life's toughest lessons without having to experience them.

Devotion #31

FINDING THE RIGHT FRIENDS

He who walks with wise men will be wise,
but the companion of fools will be destroyed.
Proverbs 13:20 NKJV

Because we tend to become like our friends, we must choose our friends carefully. Because our friends influence us in ways that are both subtle and powerful, we must ensure that our friendships honor God. Because our friends have the power to lift us up or to bring us down, we must select friends who, by their words and their actions, encourage us to lead Christ-centered lives.

When we build lasting friendships that are pleasing to God, we are blessed. When we seek out encouraging friends and mentors, they lift us up. And, when we make ourselves a powerful source of encouragement to others, we do God's work here on earth.

Do you seek to be a godly Christian? If so, you should build friendships that honor your Creator. When you do, God will bless you and your friends, today and forever.

Iron sharpens iron, and one man sharpens another.
Proverbs 27:17 HCSB

No receipt opens the heart but a true friend, to whom you may impart griefs, joys, fears, hopes, suspicions, counsels, and whatever lies upon the heart.
Francis Bacon

The best times in life are made a thousand times better when shared with a dear friend.
Luci Swindoll

In friendship, God opens your eyes to the glories of Himself.
Joni Eareckson Tada

SOMETHING TO THINK ABOUT

Put peer pressure to work for you by spending time with people who put pressure on you to become a better person.

Devotion #32

STOP, LOOK, PLAN, AND PRAY

You will seek Me and find Me
when you search for Me with all your heart.
Jeremiah 29:13 HCSB

Would you like a formula for successful living that never fails? Here it is: Include God in every aspect of your life's journey, including the plans that you make and the steps that you take. But beware: as you make plans for the days and weeks ahead, you may become sidetracked by the demands of everyday living.

If you allow the world to establish your priorities, you will eventually become discouraged or disappointed, or both. But if you genuinely seek God's will for every important decision that you make, your loving Heavenly Father will guide your steps and enrich your life. So as you plan your work, remember that every good plan should start with God, including yours.

He granted their request because they trusted in Him.
1 Chronicles 5:20 HCSB

Allow your dreams a place in your prayers and plans.
God-given dreams can help you move
into the future He is preparing for you.
Barbara Johnson

Faith in God will not get for you everything
you want, but it will get for you what
God wants you to have. The unbeliever does not
need what he wants; the Christian should want
only what he needs.
Vance Havner

The only way you can experience abundant life
is to surrender your plans to Him.
Charles Stanley

SOMETHING TO THINK ABOUT

It isn't that complicated: If you plan your steps carefully, and if you follow your plan conscientiously, you will probably succeed. If you don't, you probably won't.

Devotion #33

CHOOSING A HEALTHY LIFESTYLE

Don't you know that you are God's sanctuary and that the Spirit of God lives in you?
1 Corinthians 3:16 HCSB

Maintaining good health is not only a common-sense exercise in personal discipline; it is also a spiritual journey ordained by our Creator. God does not intend that we abuse our bodies by giving in to excessive appetites or to lazy behavior. To the contrary, God instructs us to protect our physical bodies—to do otherwise is to disobey Him.

God has a plan for every aspect of your life, and His plan includes provisions for your spiritual, physical, and emotional health. But, He expects you to do your fair share of the work!

In a world that is chock-full of temptations, you may find it all too easy to make unhealthy choices. Your challenge, of course, is to resist those unhealthy temptations by every means you can, including prayer. And of this you can be sure: when you ask for God's help, He will give it.

Therefore, brothers, by the mercies of God,
I urge you to present your bodies as a living sacrifice,
holy and pleasing to God; this is your spiritual worship.
Romans 12:1 HCSB

If you desire to improve your physical well-being
and your emotional outlook,
increasing your faith can help you.
John Maxwell

Jesus Christ is the One by Whom, for Whom,
through Whom everything was made.
Therefore, He knows what's wrong
in your life and how to fix it.
Anne Graham Lotz

God wants you to give Him your body.
Some people do foolish things with their bodies.
God wants your body as a holy sacrifice.
Warren Wiersbe

SOMETHING TO THINK ABOUT

One of the wisest choices you can make is the choice to take care of your body. That means saying "Yes" to a healthy lifestyle and "No" to any substance that has the potential to harm you.

Devotion #34

YOUR CHOICES MATTER

But seek first the kingdom of God and His righteousness, and all these things shall be added to you.
Matthew 6:33 NKJV

Life is a series of choices. From the instant we wake in the morning until the moment we nod off to sleep at night, we make countless decisions: decisions about the things we do, decisions about the words we speak, and decisions about the thoughts we choose to think. Simply put, the quality of those decisions determines the quality of our lives.

As believers who have been saved by a loving and merciful God, we have every reason to make wise choices. Yet sometimes, amid the inevitable hustle and bustle of life here on earth, we allow ourselves to behave in ways that we know are displeasing to God. When we do, we forfeit—albeit temporarily—the joy and the peace that we might otherwise experience through Him.

As you consider the next step in your life's journey, take time to consider how many things in this life you can control: your thoughts, your words, your priorities, and your actions, for starters. And then, if you sincerely want to discover God's purpose for your life, make choices that are pleasing to Him.

MORE FROM GOD'S WORD ABOUT YOUR CHOICES

I have set before you life and death, blessing and curse. Choose life so that you and your descendants may live, love the Lord your God, obey Him, and remain faithful to Him. For He is your life, and He will prolong your life in the land the Lord swore to give to your fathers Abraham, Isaac, and Jacob.

Deuteronomy 30:19-20 HCSB

Don't be deceived: God is not mocked. For whatever a man sows he will also reap, because the one who sows to his flesh will reap corruption from the flesh, but the one who sows to the Spirit will reap eternal life from the Spirit.

Galatians 6:7-8 HCSB

Therefore, get your minds ready for action, being self-disciplined, and set your hope completely on the grace to be brought to you at the revelation of Jesus Christ. As obedient children, do not be conformed to the desires of your former ignorance but, as the One who called you is holy, you also are to be holy in all your conduct.

1 *Peter* 1:13-15 HCSB

Lead a tranquil and quiet life in all godliness and dignity.

1 *Timothy* 2:2 HCSB

No matter how many books you read, no matter how many schools you attend, you're never really wise until you start making wise choices.
Marie T. Freeman

Commitment to His lordship on Easter, at revivals, or even every Sunday is not enough. We must choose this day—and every day—whom we will serve. This deliberate act of the will is the inevitable choice between habitual fellowship and habitual failure.
Beth Moore

Life is a series of choices between the bad, the good, and the best. Everything depends on how we choose.
Vance Havner

SOMETHING TO THINK ABOUT

Every step of your life's journey is a choice . . . and the quality of those choices determines the quality of the journey.

Devotion #35

THE DECISION TO BE THANKFUL

Give thanks to the Lord, for He is good;
His faithful love endures forever.
Psalm 106:1 HCSB

Sometimes, life can be complicated, demanding, and busy. When the demands of life leave us rushing from place to place with scarcely a moment to spare, we may fail to pause and say a word of thanks for all the good things we've received. But when we fail to count our blessings, we rob ourselves of the happiness, the peace, and the gratitude that should rightfully be ours.

Today, even if you're busily engaged in life, slow down long enough to start counting your blessings. You most certainly will not be able to count them all, but take a few moments to jot down as many blessings as you can. Then, give thanks to the Giver of all good things: God. His love for you is eternal, as are His gifts. And it's never too soon—or too late—to offer Him thanks.

MORE FROM GOD'S WORD ABOUT THANKSGIVING

Thanks be to God for His indescribable gift.
2 Corinthians 9:15 HCSB

And let the peace of the Messiah,
to which you were also called in one body,
control your hearts. Be thankful.
Colossians 3:15 HCSB

Therefore as you have received Christ Jesus the Lord,
walk in Him, rooted and built up in Him
and established in the faith, just as you were taught,
and overflowing with thankfulness.
Colossians 2:6-7 HCSB

It is good to give thanks to the Lord,
And to sing praises to Your name, O Most High.
Psalm 92:1 NKJV

Enter into His gates with thanksgiving,
and into His courts with praise. Be thankful to Him,
and bless His name. For the Lord is good;
His mercy is everlasting, and His truth
endures to all generations.
Psalm 100:4-5 NKJV

Thanksgiving or complaining—these words express two contrastive attitudes of the souls of God's children in regard to His dealings with them. The soul that gives thanks can find comfort in everything; the soul that complains can find comfort in nothing.

Hannah Whitall Smith

It is only with gratitude that life becomes rich.

Dietrich Bonhoeffer

It is always possible to be thankful for what is given rather than to complain about what is not given. One or the other becomes a habit of life.

Elisabeth Elliot

Thanksgiving is good but Thanksliving is better.

Jim Gallery

SOMETHING TO THINK ABOUT

When is the best time to say "thanks" to God? Any time. God never takes a vacation, and He's always ready to hear from you. So what are you waiting for?

Devotion #36

ENTRUST YOUR FUTURE TO GOD

For I know the thoughts that I think toward you, says the Lord, thoughts of peace and not of evil, to give you a future and a hope. Then you will call upon Me and go and pray to Me, and I will listen to you.

Jeremiah 29:11-12 NKJV

How can you make smart choices if you're unwilling to trust God and obey Him? The answer, of course, is that you can't. That's why you should trust God in everything (and that means entrusting your future to God).

How bright is your future? Well, if you're a faithful believer, God's plans for you are so bright that you'd better wear shades. But here are some important follow-up questions: How bright do you believe your future to be? Are you expecting a terrific tomorrow, or are you dreading a terrible one? The answer you give will have a powerful impact on the way tomorrow turns out.

Do you trust in the ultimate goodness of God's plan for your life? Will you face tomorrow's challenges with optimism and hope? You should. After all, God created you for a very important reason: His reason. And you have important work to do: His work.

Today, as you live in the present and look to the future, remember that God has an amazing plan for you. Act—and believe—accordingly.

Do not boast about tomorrow, for you do not know what a day may bring forth.
Proverbs 27:1 NKJV

We must trust as if it all depended on God and work as if it all depended on us.
C. H. Spurgeon

Every man lives by faith, the nonbeliever as well as the saint; the one by faith in natural laws and the other by faith in God.
A. W. Tozer

Faith in faith is pointless.
Faith in a living, active God moves mountains.
Beth Moore

SOMETHING TO THINK ABOUT

Hope for the future isn't some pie-in-the-sky dream; hope for the future is simply one aspect of trusting God.

Devotion #37

YES, YOU'RE WORTH IT!

You're blessed when you're content with just who you are—no more, no less.
That's the moment you find yourselves proud owners of everything that can't be bought.
Matthew 5:5 MSG

How many people in the world are exactly like you? The only person in the world who's exactly like you . . . IS YOU! And that means you're special: special to God, special to your family, special to your friends, and a special addition to God's wonderful world.

But sometimes, when you are tired, angry, dejected, or depressed, you may not feel very special. In fact, you may decide that you're the ugliest duckling in the pond, a not-very-special person . . . but whenever you think like that, you're mistaken.

So the next time that you start feeling like you don't measure up, remember this: when God made all the people of the earth, He only made one you. You're incredibly valuable to God, and that means you should think of yourself as a V.I.P. (a Very Important Person). God wants you to have the best, and you deserve the best . . . you're worth it!

Happy is he who does not condemn himself . . . .
Romans 14:22 NASB

You are valuable just because you exist.
Not because of what you do or what you have done,
but simply because you are.
Max Lucado

Human worth does not depend on beauty or
intelligence or accomplishments. We are all more
valuable than the possessions of the entire world
simply because God gave us that value.
James Dobson

Being loved by Him whose opinion matters
most gives us the security to risk loving, too—
even loving ourselves.
Gloria Gaither

SOMETHING TO THINK ABOUT

Don't be too hard on yourself: you don't have to be perfect to be wonderful.

Devotion #38

THE POWER OF FAITH

Believe in the Lord your God,
and you will be established; believe in His prophets,
and you will succeed.
2 Chronicles 20:20 HCSB

In the months and years ahead, your faith will be tested many times. Every life—including yours—is a series of successes and failures, celebrations and disappointments, joys and sorrows. Every step of the way, through every triumph and tragedy, God will stand by your side and strengthen you . . . if you have faith in Him. Jesus taught His disciples that if they had faith, they could move mountains. You can too.

If you place your faith, your trust, indeed your life in the hands of Christ Jesus, you'll be amazed at the marvelous things He can do with you and through you. Faith is a willingness to believe in things that are unseeable and to trust in things that are unknowable.

Today and every day, strengthen your faith through praise, through worship, through Bible study, and through prayer. God has big plans for you, so trust His plans and strengthen your faith in Him. With God, all things are possible, and He stands ready to help you accomplish miraculous things with your life . . . if you have faith.

Now without faith it is impossible to please God,
for the one who draws near to Him must believe
that He exists and rewards those who seek Him.
Hebrews 11:6 HCSB

Faith does not concern itself with
the entire journey. One step is enough.
Mrs. Charles E. Cowman

There are a lot of things in life that are
difficult to understand. Faith allows the soul to go
beyond what the eyes can see.
John Maxwell

Do something that demonstrates faith,
for faith with no effort is no faith at all.
Max Lucado

SOMETHING TO THINK ABOUT

If your faith is strong enough, you and God—working together—can move mountains.

Devotion #39

THE DIRECTION OF YOUR THOUGHTS

Finally brothers, whatever is true,
whatever is honorable, whatever is just,
whatever is pure, whatever is lovely,
whatever is commendable—if there is
any moral excellence and if there is any praise—
dwell on these things.
Philippians 4:8 HCSB

How will you direct your thoughts today? Will you obey the words of Philippians 4:8 by dwelling upon those things that are honorable, true, and worthy of praise? Or will you allow your thoughts to be hijacked by the negativity that seems to dominate our troubled world?

Are you fearful, angry, bored, or worried? Are you so preoccupied with the concerns of this day that you fail to thank God for the promise of eternity? Are you confused, bitter, or pessimistic? If so, God wants to have a little talk with you. He wants to remind you of His infinite love and His boundless grace. As you contemplate these things, and as you give thanks for God's blessings, negativity should no longer dominate your day or your life.

MORE FROM GOD'S WORD ABOUT YOUR THOUGHTS

Set your minds on what is above,
not on what is on the earth.
Colossians 3:2 HCSB

Commit your works to the Lord,
and your thoughts will be established.
Proverbs 16:3 NKJV

Brothers, don't be childish in your thinking,
but be infants in evil and adult in your thinking.
1 Corinthians 14:20 HCSB

Guard your heart above all else,
for it is the source of life.
Proverbs 4:23 HCSB

May the words of my mouth and the meditation of
my heart be acceptable to You, Lord,
my rock and my Redeemer.
Psalm 19:14 HCSB

Your thoughts are the determining factor
as to whose mold you are conformed to.
Control your thoughts and you control
the direction of your life.
Charles Stanley

I became aware of one very important concept
I had missed before: my attitude—
not my circumstances—
was what was making me unhappy.
Vonette Bright

Attitude is the mind's paintbrush;
it can color any situation.
Barbara Johnson

SOMETHING TO THINK ABOUT

You have the power to choose the direction of your thoughts. Good thoughts lead to good results; bad thoughts lead elsewhere.

Devotion #40

PRIORITIES THAT ARE PLEASING TO GOD

Draw near to God,
and He will draw near to you.
James 4:8 HCSB

Have you fervently asked God to help prioritize your life? Have you asked Him for guidance and for the courage to do the things that you know need to be done? If so, then you're continually inviting your Creator to reveal Himself in a variety of ways. As a follower of Christ, you must do no less.

When you make God's priorities your priorities, you will receive God's abundance and His peace. When you make God a full partner in every aspect of your life, He will lead you along the proper path: His path. When you allow God to reign over your heart, He will honor you with spiritual blessings that are simply too numerous to count. So, as you plan for the day ahead, make God's will your ultimate priority. When you do, every other priority will have a tendency to fall neatly into place.

MORE FROM GOD'S WORD ABOUT PRIORITIES

So teach us to number our days,
that we may gain a heart of wisdom.
Psalm 90:12 NKJV

For where your treasure is,
there your heart will be also.
Luke 12:34 HCSB

Come to Me, all you who are weary and burdened, and I will give you rest. Take My yoke upon you and learn from Me, because I am gentle and humble in heart, and you will find rest for your souls. For My yoke is easy and My burden is light.
Matthew 11:28–30 HCSB

The result of righteousness will be peace;
the effect of righteousness will be
quiet confidence forever.
Isaiah 32:17 HCSB

If you love Me, you will keep My commandments.
John 14:15 HCSB

In the name of Jesus Christ who was never in a hurry, we pray, O God, that You will slow us down, for we know that we live too fast. With all eternity before us, make us take time to live—time to get acquainted with You, time to enjoy Your blessing, and time to know each other.

Peter Marshall

Give God what's right—not what's left!

Quips, Anonymous

With God, it's never "Plan B" or "second best." It's always "Plan A." And, if we let Him, He'll make something beautiful of our lives.

Gloria Gaither

SOMETHING TO THINK ABOUT

Setting priorities may mean saying no. You don't have time to do everything, so it's perfectly okay to say no to the things that mean less so that you'll have time for the things that mean more.

Devotion #41

THE WORDS YOU SPEAK

I tell you that on the day of judgment people
will have to account for every careless word they speak.
For by your words you will be acquitted,
and by your words you will be condemned.
Matthew 12:36-37 HCSB

This world can be a difficult place, a place where many of our friends and family members are troubled by the inevitable challenges of everyday life. And since we can never be certain who needs our help, we should be careful to speak helpful words to everybody who crosses our paths.

In the book of Ephesians, Paul writes, "Do not let any unwholesome talk come out of your mouths, but only what is helpful for building others up according to their needs, that it may benefit those who listen" (4:29 NIV). Paul reminds us that when we choose our words carefully, we can have a powerful impact on those around us.

Today, let's share kind words, smiles, encouragement, and hugs with family, with friends, and with the world.

Pleasant words are a honeycomb:
sweet to the taste and health to the body.
Proverbs 16:24 HCSB

I still believe we ought to talk about Jesus. The old country doctor of my boyhood days always began his examination by saying, "Let me see your tongue." That's a good way to check a Christian: the tongue test. Let's hear what he is talking about.
Vance Havner

When you talk, choose the very same words that you would use if Jesus were looking over your shoulder. Because He is.
Marie T. Freeman

The great test of a man's character is his tongue.
Oswald Chambers

SOMETHING TO THINK ABOUT

If you're tempted to be critical of others, remember that your ability to judge others requires a level of insight that you simply don't have. So do everybody (including yourself) a favor: don't criticize.

Devotion #42

ON THE ROAD AHEAD, CHOOSE WISE ROLE MODELS

A wise man will hear and increase learning,
and a man of understanding
will attain wise counsel.
Proverbs 1:5 NKJV

Here's a simple yet effective way to strengthen your faith: Choose role models whose faith in God is strong.

When you emulate godly people, you become a more godly person yourself. That's why you should seek out mentors who, by their words and their presence, make you a better person and a better Christian.

Today, as a gift to yourself, select, from your friends and family members, a mentor whose judgement you trust. Then listen carefully to your mentor's advice and be willing to accept that advice, even if accepting it requires effort or pain, or both. Consider your mentor to be God's gift to you. Thank God for that gift, and use it for the glory of His kingdom.

Listen, my son, to your father's instruction
and do not forsake your mother's teaching.
Proverbs 1:8 NIV

The effective mentor strives to help a man or
woman discover what they can be in Christ
and then holds them accountable
to become that person.
Howard Hendricks

Yes, the Spirit was sent to be our Counselor.
Yes, Jesus speaks to us personally.
But often he works through another human being.
John Eldredge

It takes a wise person to give good advice,
but an even wiser person to take it.
Marie T. Freeman

SOMETHING TO THINK ABOUT

Talk to the experts: Your mentors may not have all of the answers, but at least they'll know most of the questions! So ask, listen, and learn.

Devotion #43

BEING A CHEERFUL CHRISTIAN

A cheerful heart has a continual feast.
Proverbs 15:15 HCSB

Few things in life are more sad, or, for that matter, more absurd, than a grumpy Christian. Christ promises us lives of abundance and joy, but He does not force His joy upon us. We must claim His joy for ourselves, and when we do, Jesus, in turn, fills our spirits with His power and His love.

How can we receive from Christ the joy that is rightfully ours? By giving Him what is rightfully His: our hearts and our souls.

When we earnestly commit ourselves to the Savior of mankind, when we place Jesus at the center of our lives and trust Him as our personal Savior, He will transform us, not just for today, but for all eternity. Then we, as God's children, can share Christ's joy and His message with a world that needs both.

A joyful heart makes a face cheerful.
Proverbs 15:13 HCSB

God is good, and heaven is forever.
And if those two facts don't cheer you up,
nothing will.
Marie T. Freeman

Sour godliness is the devil's religion.
John Wesley

The people whom I have seen succeed best in life
have always been cheerful and hopeful people
who went about their business
with a smile on their faces.
Charles Kingsley

SOMETHING TO THINK ABOUT

Do you need a little cheering up? If so, find somebody else who needs cheering up, too. Then, do your best to brighten that person's day. When you do, you'll discover that cheering up other people is a wonderful way to cheer yourself up, too!

Devotion #44

LET GOD GUIDE THE WAY

In all your ways acknowledge Him,
and He shall direct your paths.
Proverbs 3:6 NKJV

The Bible promises that God will guide you if you let Him. Your job is to let Him. But sometimes, you will be tempted to do otherwise. Sometimes, you'll be tempted to go along with the crowd; other times, you'll be tempted to do things your way, not God's way. When you feel these temptations, resist them.

God has promised that when you ask for His help, He will not withhold it. So ask. Ask Him to meet the needs of your day. Ask Him to lead you, to protect you, and to correct you. And trust the answers He gives.

God stands at the door and waits. When you knock, He opens. When you ask, He answers. Your task, of course, is to seek His guidance prayerfully, confidently, and often.

Lord, You light my lamp;
my God illuminates my darkness.
Psalm 18:28 HCSB

We must always invite Jesus to be the navigator of
our plans, desires, wills, and emotions,
for He is the way, the truth, and the life.
Bill Bright

God often reveals His direction for our lives
through the way He made us . . .
with a certain personality and unique skills.
Bill Hybels

God's leading will never be contrary to His word.
Vonette Bright

SOMETHING TO THINK ABOUT

If you're wise, you'll allow God to guide you today and every day of your life. When you pray for guidance, God will give it.

Devotion #45

AVOID PEOPLE WHO BEHAVE FOOLISHLY

Do not be deceived:
"Bad company corrupts good morals."
1 Corinthians 15:33 HCSB

If you associate with people who do foolish things, pretty soon, you'll probably find yourself doing foolish things, too. And that's bad . . . very bad. So here's an ironclad rule for earning more self-respect and more rewards from life: If your peer group is headed in the wrong direction, find another peer group, and fast. Otherwise, before you know it, you'll be caught up in trouble that you didn't create and you don't deserve.

When you feel pressured to do things—or to say things—that lead you away from God, you're heading straight for trouble. So don't do the "easy" thing or the "popular" thing. Do the right thing, and don't worry about winning any popularity contests.

Stay away from a foolish man;
you will gain no knowledge from his speech.
Proverbs 14:7 HCSB

Inasmuch as anyone pushes you nearer to God,
he or she is your friend.
Barbara Johnson

True friends don't spend time gazing into each other's eyes. They show great tenderness toward each other, but they face in the same direction, toward common projects, interest, goals, and above all, toward a common Lord.
C. S. Lewis

We, as God's people, are not only to stay far away from sin and sinners who would entice us, but we are to be so like our God that we mourn over sin.
Kay Arthur

SOMETHING TO THINK ABOUT

Take time to think about ways that you can remove yourself from situations that might compromise your integrity.

Devotion #46

TACKLING TOUGH TIMES

God is our refuge and strength,
a helper who is always found in times of trouble.
Psalm 46:1 HCSB

As we travel the roads of life, all of us are confronted with streets that seem to be dead-ends. When we do, we may become discouraged. After all, we live in a society where expectations can be high and demands even higher.

If you find yourself having to endure difficult circumstances, remember that God remains in His heaven. If you become discouraged with the direction of your day or your life, turn your thoughts and prayers to Him. He is a God of possibility, not negativity. He will guide you through your difficulties and beyond them. And then, with a renewed spirit of optimism and hope, you can thank the Giver of all things good for gifts that are simply too profound to fully understand and for treasures that are too numerous to count.

I will be with you when you pass through the waters . . .
when you walk through the fire . . . the flame will not
burn you. For I the Lord your God,
the Holy One of Israel, and your Savior.
Isaiah 43:2-3 HCSB

Jesus does not say, "There is no storm."
He says, "I am here, do not toss, but trust."
Vance Havner

Your greatest ministry will likely
come out of your greatest hurt.
Rick Warren

Measure the size of the obstacles against
the size of God.
Beth Moore

SOMETHING TO THINK ABOUT

Talk about it! If you're having tough times, don't hit the panic button and don't keep everything bottled up inside. Talk things over with people you can really trust. And if your troubles seem overwhelming, be willing to seek help—starting, of course, with your parents and your pastor.

Devotion #47

FIND WORTHWHILE THINGS YOU CAN BE PASSIONATE ABOUT

Whatever you do,
do all to the glory of God.
1 Corinthians 10:31 NKJV

We all need to discover a purpose for our lives, a purpose that excites us and causes us to live each day with passion.

Anna Quindlen had this advice: "Consider the lilies of the field. Look at the fuzz on a baby's ear. Read in the backyard with the sun on your face. Learn to be happy. And think of life as a terminal illness, because, if you do, you will live it with joy and passion, as it ought to be lived."

If you have not yet discovered a passionate pursuit that blesses you and your world, don't allow yourself to become discouraged. Instead, keep searching and keep trusting that with God's help, you can—and will—find a meaningful way to serve your neighbors, your Creator, and yourself.

In all the work you are doing, work the best you can.
Work as if you were doing it for the Lord,
not for people.
Colossians 3:23 NCV

Some of us simmer all our lives
and never come to a boil.
Vance Havner

When we wholeheartedly commit ourselves to God, there is nothing mediocre or run-of-the-mill about us. To live for Christ is to be passionate about our Lord and about our lives.
Jim Gallery

Am I ignitable? God deliver me from the dread asbestos of "other things." Saturate me with the oil of the Spirit that I may be aflame.
Jim Elliot

SOMETHING TO THINK ABOUT

Involve yourself in activities that you can support wholeheartedly and enthusiastically. It's easier to celebrate life when you're passionately involved in life.

Devotion #48

PRAY EARLY AND OFTEN

Rejoice always! Pray constantly.
Give thanks in everything,
for this is God's will for you in Christ Jesus.
1 Thessalonians 5:16-18 HCSB

Perhaps, because of your demanding schedule, you've neglected to pay sufficient attention to a particularly important part of your life: the spiritual part. If so, today is the day to change, and one way to make that change is simply to spend a little more time talking with God.

Perhaps, on occasion, you may find yourself overwhelmed by the press of everyday life. Perhaps you may forget to slow yourself down long enough to talk with God. Instead of turning your thoughts and prayers to Him, you may rely upon your own resources. Instead of asking God for guidance, you may depend only upon your own limited wisdom. A far better course of action is this: simply stop what you're doing long enough to open your heart to God; then listen carefully for His directions.

In all things great and small, seek God's wisdom and His grace. He hears your prayers, and He will answer. All you must do is ask.

The intense prayer of the righteous is very powerful.
James 5:16 HCSB

Some people pray just to pray,
and some people pray to know God.
Andrew Murray

We are not to have faith in prayer,
but in God who answers prayer.
Anonymous

Pour out your heart to God and tell Him
how you feel. Be real, be honest,
and when you get it all out, you'll start
to feel the gradual covering of
God's comforting presence.
Bill Hybels

SOMETHING TO THINK ABOUT

When you are praying, the position of your eyelids makes little or no difference. Of course it's good to close your eyes and bow your head whenever you can, but it's also good to offer quick prayers to God with your eyes—and your heart—wide open.

Devotion #49

FACING UP TO YOUR RESPONSIBILITIES

Now we want each of you to demonstrate
the same diligence for the final realization of your hope,
so that you won't become lazy,
but imitators of those who inherit the promises
through faith and perseverance.
Hebrews 6:11-12 HCSB

The words from the sixth chapter of Hebrews remind us that as Christians we must labor diligently, patiently, and faithfully. Do you want to be a worthy example for your family and friends? If so, you must preach the gospel of responsible behavior, not only with your words, but also by your actions.

It's not always easy to face up to your responsibilities, but it's always the right thing to do. So the next time you're faced with the choice of doing the right thing or the easy thing, do what's right. It's the truly decent way to live.

So then each of us shall give account of himself to God.
Romans 14:12 NKJV

Whether we know it or not, whether we agree with it or not, whether we practice it or not, whether we like it or not, we are accountable to one another.
Charles Stanley

Every time you refuse to face up to life and its problems, you weaken your character.
E. Stanley Jones

Jesus knows one of the greatest barriers to our faith is often our unwillingness to be made whole—our unwillingness to accept responsibility—our unwillingness to live without excuse for our spiritual smallness and immaturity.
Anne Graham Lotz

SOMETHING TO THINK ABOUT

When you accept responsibilities and fulfill them, you'll feel better about yourself. When you avoid your obligations, you won't. Act accordingly.

Devotion #50

THE CHOICE TO KNOW JESUS

Then Jesus spoke to them again, saying, "I am the light of the world. He who follows Me shall not walk in darkness, but have the light of life."
John 8:12 NKJV

There's really no way around it: If you want to know God, you've got to get to know His Son. And that's good, because getting to know Jesus can—and should—be the most enriching experience of your life.

Can you honestly say that you're passionate about your faith and that you're really following Jesus? Hopefully so. But if you're preoccupied with other things—or if you're strictly a one-day-a-week Christian—then you're in need of a major-league spiritual makeover.

Jesus doesn't want you to be a lukewarm believer; Jesus wants you to be a "new creation" through Him. And that's exactly what you should want for yourself, too. Nothing is more important than your wholehearted commitment to your Creator and to His only begotten Son. Your faith must never be an afterthought; it must be your ultimate priority, your ultimate possession, and your ultimate passion.

Love consists in this: not that we loved God,
but that He loved us and sent His Son
to be the propitiation for our sins.
1 John 4:10 HCSB

Jesus is not a strong man making men and women
who gather around Him weak.
He is the Strong creating the strong.
E. Stanley Jones

Think of this—we may live together with Him
here and now, a daily walking with Him
who loved us and gave Himself for us.
Elisabeth Elliot

To walk out of His will is to walk into nowhere.
C. S. Lewis

SOMETHING TO THINK ABOUT

When Jesus endured His sacrifice on the cross, He paid a terrible price for you. What price are you willing to pay for Him?

Devotion #51

YOUR BEHAVIOR MATTERS

As God's slaves, live as free people, but don't use your freedom as a way to conceal evil.
1 Peter 2:16 HCSB

For most of us, it is a daunting thought: one day, perhaps soon, we'll come face to face with our Heavenly Father, and we'll be called to account for our actions here on earth. Our personal histories will certainly not be surprising to God; He already knows everything about us. But the full scope of our activities may be surprising to us: some of us will be pleasantly surprised; others will not be.

Today, as you begin the next stage of your life's journey, do whatever you can to ensure that your thoughts and your deeds are pleasing to your Creator. Because you will, at some point in the future, be called to account for your actions. And the future may be sooner than you think.

MORE FROM GOD'S WORD ABOUT HOW YOU SHOULD BEHAVE

Therefore, get your minds ready for action, being self-disciplined, and set your hope completely on the grace to be brought to you at the revelation of Jesus Christ. As obedient children, do not be conformed to the desires of your former ignorance but, as the One who called you is holy, you also are to be holy in all your conduct.
1 Peter 1:13-15 HCSB

Lead a tranquil and quiet life in all godliness and dignity.
1 Timothy 2:2 HCSB

For this very reason, make every effort to supplement your faith with goodness, goodness with knowledge, knowledge with self-control, self-control with endurance, endurance with godliness.
2 Peter 1:5-6 HCSB

Therefore as you have received Christ Jesus the Lord, walk in Him.
Colossians 2:6 HCSB

Although our actions have nothing to do
with gaining our own salvation, they might be used
by God to save somebody else!
What we do really matters, and it can affect
the eternities of people we care about.
Bill Hybels

Nobody is good by accident.
No man ever became holy by chance.
C. H. Spurgeon

Either God's Word keeps you from sin,
or sin keeps you from God's Word.
Corrie ten Boom

SOMETHING TO THINK ABOUT

Ask yourself if your behavior has been radically changed by your unfolding relationship with God. If the answer to this question is unclear to you—or if the honest answer is a resounding no—think of a single step you can take, a positive change in your life, that will bring you closer to your Creator.

Devotion #52

THE RIGHT KIND OF FEAR

Therefore, since we are receiving a kingdom
that cannot be shaken, let us hold on to grace.
By it, we may serve God acceptably,
with reverence and awe.
Hebrews 12:28 HCSB

Do you have a healthy, fearful respect for God's power? If so, you are both wise and obedient. And, because you are a thoughtful believer, you also understand that genuine wisdom begins with a profound appreciation for God's limitless power.

God praises humility and punishes pride. That's why God's greatest servants will always be those humble men and women who care less for their own glory and more for God's glory. In God's kingdom, the only way to achieve greatness is to shun it. And the only way to be wise is to understand these facts: God is great; He is all-knowing; and He is all-powerful. We must respect Him, and we must humbly obey His commandments, or we must accept the consequences of our misplaced pride.

To fear the Lord is to hate evil.
Proverbs 8:13 HCSB

It is not possible that mortal men should be thoroughly conscious of the divine presence without being filled with awe.
C. H. Spurgeon

The remarkable thing about fearing God is that when you fear God, you fear nothing else, whereas if you do not fear God, you fear everything else.
Oswald Chambers

A healthy fear of God will do much to deter us from sin.
Charles Swindoll

SOMETHING TO THINK ABOUT

The fear of God is the right kind of fear: Your respect for God should make you fearful of disobeying Him . . . very fearful.

Devotion #53

BE PATIENT WITH OTHERS AND WITH YOURSELF

Therefore, God's chosen ones,
holy and loved, put on heartfelt compassion,
kindness, humility, gentleness, and patience.
Colossians 3:12 HCSB

The dictionary defines the word *patience* as "the ability to be calm, tolerant, and understanding." If that describes you, you can skip the rest of this page. But, if you're like most of us, you'd better keep reading.

For most of us, patience is a hard thing to master. Why? Because we have lots of things we want, and we want them NOW (if not sooner). But the Bible tells us that we must learn to wait patiently for the things that God has in store for us.

The next time you find your patience tested to the limit, remember that the world unfolds according to God's timetable, not yours. Sometimes, you must wait patiently, and that's as it should be. After all, think about how patient God has been with you!

Be gentle to everyone, able to teach, and patient.
2 Timothy 2:23 HCSB

We must never think that patience is complacency.
Patience is endurance in action.
Warren Wiersbe

If only we could be as patient
with other people as God is with us!
Jim Gallery

A keen sense of humor helps us to overlook the unbecoming, understand the unconventional, tolerate the unpleasant, overcome the unexpected, and outlast the unbearable.
Billy Graham

SOMETHING TO THINK ABOUT

If you want your friends to be patient with you, then you must do the same for them. Never expect other people to be more patient with you than you are with them.

Devotion #54

LOOK FOR MIRACLES

Is anything impossible for the Lord?
Genesis 18:14 HCSB

One way to know more about God is to look carefully at the miraculous things that He does. But sometimes, we're simply too preoccupied to notice. Instead of paying careful attention to God's handiwork, we become distracted. Instead of expecting God to work miracles, we become cynical. Instead of depending on God's awesome power, we seek to muddle along using our own power—with decidedly mixed results.

Miracles, both great and small, are an integral part of everyday life—and they are a part of your life, too. But here's the million-dollar question: have you noticed?

For nothing will be impossible with God.
Luke 1:37 HCSB

When God is involved, anything can happen.
Be open and stay that way. God has a beautiful way
of bringing good vibrations out of broken chords.
Charles Swindoll

Miracles broke the physical laws of the universe;
forgiveness broke the moral rules.
Philip Yancey

I could go through this day oblivious to
the miracles all around me
or I could tune in and "enjoy."
Gloria Gaither

SOMETHING TO THINK ABOUT

God is in the business of doing miraculous things. Are you in the habit of asking Him to do miraculous things in your life?

Devotion #55

DON'T WORSHIP THE WORLD

For to be carnally minded is death,
but to be spiritually minded is life and peace.
Romans 8:6 NKJV

We live in the world, but we must not worship it. Our duty is to place God first and everything else second. But because we are fallible beings with imperfect faith, placing God in His rightful place is often difficult. In fact, at every turn, or so it seems, we are tempted to do otherwise.

Our world can be a noisy, distracting place filled with countless opportunities to stray from God's will. The world seems to cry, "Worship me with your time, your money, your energy, and your thoughts!" But God commands otherwise: He commands us to worship Him and Him alone; everything else must be secondary.

MORE FROM GOD'S WORD ABOUT WORLDLINESS

Pure and undefiled religion before our God and Father is this: to look after orphans and widows in their distress and to keep oneself unstained by the world.

James 1:27 HCSB

Now we have not received the spirit of the world, but the Spirit who is from God, in order to know what has been freely given to us by God.

1 Corinthians 2:12 HCSB

No one should deceive himself. If anyone among you thinks he is wise in this age, he must become foolish so that he can become wise. For the wisdom of this world is foolishness with God, since it is written: He catches the wise in their craftiness.

1 Corinthians 3:18-19 HCSB

Do not love the world or the things that belong to the world. If anyone loves the world, love for the Father is not in him.

1 John 2:15 HCSB

Jesus calls you to be a non-conformist.
Live to be separated from the evils of the world.
Live to be different.
Billy Graham

The only ultimate disaster that can befall us,
I have come to realize, is to feel ourselves
to be home on earth.
Max Lucado

The true Christian, though he is in revolt against
the world's efforts to brainwash him,
is no mere rebel for rebellion's sake.
He dissents from the world because he knows
that it cannot make good on its promises.
A. W. Tozer

SOMETHING TO THINK ABOUT

Whose messages will you trust? If you dwell on the world's messages, you're setting yourself up for disaster. If you dwell on God's message, you're setting yourself up for victory.

Devotion #56

CHOOSING TO BE HAPPY

I have learned to be content
in whatever circumstances I am.
Philippians 4:11 HCSB

When will you celebrate God's marvelous creation? Today or tomorrow? When will you make the choice to rejoice, now or later? When will you accept the happiness and peace that can (and should) be yours—in the present moment or in the distant future? The answer to these questions is straightforward: the best moment to accept God's gifts is the present one.

Will you accept God's blessings now or later? Are you willing to give Him your full attention today? Hopefully so. He deserves it. And so, for that matter, do you.

A joyful heart is good medicine,
but a broken spirit dries up the bones.
Proverbs 17:22 HCSB

The secret of a happy life is to delight in duty.
When duty becomes delight,
then burdens become blessings.
Warren Wiersbe

I became aware of one very important concept
I had missed before: my attitude—
not my circumstances—
was what was making me unhappy.
Vonette Bright

We will never be happy until we make God
the source of our fulfillment
and the answer to our longings.
Stormie Omartian

SOMETHING TO THINK ABOUT

To make happiness last, we must obey God while celebrating His blessings. To make happiness disappear, we need only disobey God while ignoring His blessings.

Devotion #57

CHOOSING TO BE MODERATE

Moderation is better than muscle,
self-control better than political power.
Proverbs 16:32 MSG

Moderation and wisdom are traveling companions. If we are wise, we must learn to temper our appetites, our desires, and our impulses. When we do, we are blessed, in part, because God has created a world in which temperance is rewarded and intemperance is inevitably punished.

Would you like to improve your life? Then harness your appetites and restrain your impulses. Moderation is difficult, of course; it is especially difficult in a prosperous society such as ours. But the rewards of moderation are numerous and long-lasting. Claim those rewards today.

No one can force you to moderate your appetites. The decision to live temperately (and wisely) is yours and yours alone. And so are the consequences.

Be on your guard, so that your minds are not dulled from carousing, drunkenness, and worries of life.
Luke 21:34 HCSB

When I feel like circumstances are spiraling downward in my life, God taught me that whether I'm right side up or upside down, I need to turn those circumstances over to Him. He is the only one who can bring balance into my life.
Carole Lewis

Virtue—even attempted virtue—brings light; indulgence brings fog.
C. S. Lewis

To many, total abstinence is easier than perfect moderation.
St. Augustine

SOMETHING TO THINK ABOUT

When in doubt, be moderate. Moderation is wisdom in action.

Devotion #58

THE POWER OF ENCOURAGEMENT

Iron sharpens iron,
and one man sharpens another.
Proverbs 27:17 HCSB

Life is a team sport, and all of us need occasional pats on the back from our teammates. As Christians, we are called upon to spread the Good News of Christ, and we are also called to spread a message of encouragement and hope to the world.

Whether you realize it or not, many people with whom you come in contact every day are in desperate need of a smile or an encouraging word. The world can be a difficult place, and countless friends and family members may be troubled by the challenges of everyday life. Since you don't always know who needs your help, the best strategy is to try to encourage all the people who cross your path. So today, be a world-class source of encouragement to everyone you meet. Never has the need been greater.

And let us be concerned about one another in order to promote love and good works.
Hebrews 10:24 HCSB

A lot of people have gone further than they thought they could because someone else thought they could.
Zig Ziglar

In each of my friends there is something that only some other friend can fully bring out. By myself I am not large enough to call the whole man into activity; I want other lights than my own to show all his facets.
C. S. Lewis

Always stay connected to people and seek out things that bring you joy. Dream with abandon. Pray confidently.
Barbara Johnson

SOMETHING TO THINK ABOUT

Encouragement is contagious. You can't lift other people up without lifting yourself up, too.

Devotion #59

TRUTH WITH A CAPITAL T

You will know the truth,
and the truth will set you free.
John 8:32 HCSB

God is vitally concerned with truth. His Word teaches the truth; His Spirit reveals the truth; His Son leads us to the truth. When we open our hearts to God, and when we allow His Son to rule over our thoughts and our lives, God reveals Himself, and we come to understand the truth about ourselves and the Truth (with a capital T) about God's gift of grace.

The familiar words of John 8:32 remind us that when we come to know God's Truth, we are liberated. Have you been liberated by that Truth? And are you living in accordance with the eternal truths that you find in God's Holy Word? Hopefully so.

Today, as you fulfill the responsibilities that God has placed before you, ask yourself this question: "Do my thoughts and actions bear witness to the ultimate Truth that God has placed in my heart, or am I allowing the pressures of everyday life to overwhelm me?" It's a profound question that deserves an answer . . . now.

These are the things you must do:
Speak truth to one another; render honest
and peaceful judgments in your gates.
Zechariah 8:16 HCSB

Let everything perish!
Dismiss these empty vanities!
And let us take up the search for the truth.
St. Augustine

We must go out and live among them,
manifesting the gentle, loving spirit of our Lord.
We need to make friends before
we can hope to make converts.
Lottie Moon

Those who walk in truth walk in liberty.
Beth Moore

SOMETHING TO THINK ABOUT

It's not enough to hear God's truth, or even to understand it. If you're serious about your faith, you must allow yourself to be transformed by God's truth.

Devotion #60

OPEN YOUR HEART TO GOD

He said to him, "You shall love the Lord your God
with all your heart, with all your soul,
and with all your mind.
This is the greatest and most important commandment."
Matthew 22:37-38 HCSB

If you want to know God in a more meaningful way, you'll need to open up your heart and let Him in.

C. S. Lewis observed, "A person's spiritual health is exactly proportional to his love for God." If you hope to receive a full measure of God's spiritual blessings, you must invite your Creator to rule over your heart. When you honor God in this way, His love expands to fill your heart and bless your life.

St. Augustine wrote, "I love you, Lord, not doubtingly, but with absolute certainty. Your Word beat upon my heart until I fell in love with you, and now the universe and everything in it tells me to love you."

Today, open your heart to the Father. And let your obedience be a fitting response to His never-ending love.

We love Him because He first loved us.
1 John 4:19 NKJV

If you want to know the will and voice of God,
you must give the time and effort to cultivate
a love relationship with Him.
That is what He wants!
Henry Blackaby

Man was created by God to know and love Him
in a permanent, personal relationship.
Anne Graham Lotz

The truth of the Gospel is intended to free us to
love God and others with our whole heart.
John Eldredge

SOMETHING TO THINK ABOUT

Because God first loved you, you should love Him. And one way that you demonstrate your love is by obeying Him.

Devotion #61

THE REWARDS OF HARD WORK

Don't work only while being watched, in order to please men, but as slaves of Christ, do God's will from your heart. Render service with a good attitude, as to the Lord and not to men.

Ephesians 6:6-7 HCSB

How does God intend for us to work? Does He intend for us to work diligently or does He, instead, reward mediocrity? The answer is obvious. God has created a world in which hard work is rewarded and sloppy work is not. Yet sometimes, we may seek ease over excellence, or we may be tempted to take shortcuts when God intends that we walk the straight and narrow path.

Today, heed God's Word by doing good work. Wherever you find yourself, whatever your job description, do your work, and do it with all your heart. When you do, you will most certainly win the recognition of your peers. But more importantly, God will bless your efforts and use you in ways that only He can understand. So do your work with focus and dedication. And leave the rest up to God.

He did it with all his heart. So he prospered.
2 Chronicles 31:21 NKJV

You can't climb the ladder of life
with your hands in your pockets.
Barbara Johnson

Thank God every morning when you get up that
you have something which must be done,
whether you like it or not. Work breeds a hundred
virtues that idleness never knows.
Charles Kingsley

Great relief and satisfaction can come from
seeking God's priorities for us in each season,
discerning what is "best" in the midst of many
noble opportunities, and pouring our most excellent
energies into those things.
Beth Moore

SOMETHING TO THINK ABOUT

Whether you realize it or not, your work always speaks for itself: So make sure that your work speaks well of your efforts.

Devotion #62

ACCEPTING GOD'S ABUNDANCE

I have come that they may have life,
and that they may have it more abundantly.
John 10:10 NKJV

God sent His Son so that mankind might enjoy the abundant life that Jesus describes in the familiar words of John 10:10. But, God's gifts are not guaranteed; they must be claimed by those who choose to follow Christ. As you plan for life after graduation, you may be asking yourself, "What kind of life does God intend for me?" The answer can be found in God's promise of abundance: those who accept that promise and live according to God's commandments are eternally blessed.

Whether or not we accept God's abundance is, of course, up to each of us. When we entrust our hearts and our days to the One who created us, we experience God's peace through the grace and sacrifice of His Son. But, when we turn our thoughts and our energies away from God's commandments, we inevitably forfeit the earthly peace and spiritual abundance that might otherwise be ours.

What is your focus today? Are you focused on God's Word and His will for your life? Or are you focused on the distractions of a difficult, temptation-filled world? If you sincerely seek the spiritual abundance that your Savior offers, then you should follow Him completely and without reservation. When you do, you will receive the love, the life, and the abundance that He has promised.

Come to terms with God and be at peace;
in this way good will come to you.
Job 22:21 HCSB

God is the giver, and we are the receivers. And His richest gifts are bestowed not upon those who do the greatest things, but upon those who accept His abundance and His grace.
Hannah Whitall Smith

The only way you can experience abundant life is to surrender your plans to Him.
Charles Stanley

SOMETHING TO THINK ABOUT

Don't miss out on God's abundance. Every day is a beautifully wrapped gift from God. Unwrap it; use it; and give thanks to the Giver.

Devotion #63

ON THE ROAD AHEAD, REMEMBER TO STAY HUMBLE

Humble yourselves therefore under the mighty hand of God, so that He may exalt you in due time, casting all your care upon Him, because He cares about you.
1 Peter 5:6-7 HCSB

On the road to spiritual growth, pride is a massive roadblock. The more prideful you are, the more difficult it is to know God. When you experience success, it's easy to puff out your chest and proclaim, "I did that!" But it's wrong.

Dietrich Bonhoeffer was correct when he observed, "It is very easy to overestimate the importance of our own achievements in comparison with what we owe others." In other words, reality breeds humility. So if you want to know God better, be humble. Otherwise, you'll be building a roadblock between you and your Creator (and that's a very bad thing to do!).

Do nothing out of rivalry or conceit, but in humility consider others as more important than yourselves.
Philippians 2:3 HCSB

Do you wish to rise? Begin by descending. You plan a tower that will pierce the clouds? Lay first the foundation of humility.
St. Augustine

The great characteristic of the saint is humility.
Oswald Chambers

Nothing sets a person so much out of the devil's reach as humility.
Jonathan Edwards

SOMETHING TO THINK ABOUT

Do you value humility above status? If so, God will smile upon your endeavors. But if you value status above humility, you're inviting God's displeasure. In short, humility pleases God; pride does not.

Devotion #64

GUARD YOUR HEART AND MIND

Guard your heart above all else,
for it is the source of life.
Proverbs 4:23 HCSB

You are near and dear to God. He loves you more than you can imagine, and He wants the very best for you. And one more thing: God wants you to guard your heart.

Every day, you are faced with choices . . . lots of them. You can do the right thing, or not. You can tell the truth, or not. You can be kind, generous, and obedient. Or not.

Today, the world will offer you countless opportunities to let down your guard and, by doing so, let the devil do his worst. So be watchful and obedient. Guard your heart by giving it to your Heavenly Father; it is safe with Him.

Blessed are the pure in heart, because they will see God.
Matthew 5:8 HCSB

Do nothing that you would not like to be doing when Jesus comes. Go no place where you would not like to be found when He returns.
Corrie ten Boom

The mind is a faculty, and magnificent one at that. But the heart is the dwelling place of our true beliefs.
John Eldredge

Prayer guards hearts and minds and causes God to bring peace out of chaos.
Beth Moore

SOMETHING TO THINK ABOUT

Every day of your life, you will be tempted to rebel against God's teachings. Your job, simply put, is to guard your heart against the darkness as you focus on the light.

Devotion #65

YOU DESERVE THE BEST

But as for you, be strong; don't be discouraged, for your work has a reward.
2 Chronicles 15:7 HCSB

Do you believe that you deserve the best, and that you can achieve the best? Or have you convinced yourself that you're a second-tier talent who'll be lucky to finish far back in the pack? Before you answer that question, remember this: God sent His Son so that you might enjoy an abundant life (John 10:10). But, God's gifts are not guaranteed—it's up to you to claim them.

As you plan for the next stage of your life's journey, promise yourself that when it comes to the important things, you won't settle for second best. And what, pray tell, are the "important things"? Your faith, your family, your health, your education, and your relationships, for starters. In each of these areas, you deserve to be a rip-roaring, top-drawer success.

So if you want to achieve the best that life has to offer, convince yourself that you have the ability to earn the rewards you desire. Become sold on yourself—sold on your opportunities, sold on your potential, sold on your abilities. If you're sold on yourself, chances are the world will soon become sold, too, and the results will be beautiful.

If God is for us, who is against us?
Romans 8:31 HCSB

If, in your working hours, you make the work your end, you will presently find yourself all unawares inside the only circle in your profession that really matters. You will be one of the sound craftsmen, and other sound craftsmen will know it.
C. S. *Lewis*

Few things fire up a person's commitment like dedication to excellence.
John Maxwell

The only people who achieve much are those who want knowledge so badly that they seek it while the conditions are still unfavorable. Favorable conditions never come.
C. S. *Lewis*

SOMETHING TO THINK ABOUT

Pay careful attention to the way that you evaluate yourself. And if you happen to be your own worst critic, it's time to reevaluate the way that you've been evaluating (got that?)

Devotion #66

CHOOSING INTEGRITY

The integrity of the upright will guide them.
Proverbs 11:3 NKJV

Would you like a time-tested, ironclad formula for success? Here it is: guard your integrity like you guard your wallet.

It has been said on many occasions and in many ways that honesty is the best policy. For Christians, it is far more important to note that honesty is God's policy. And if we are to be servants worthy of our Savior, Jesus Christ, we must be honest, forthright, and trustworthy.

Telling the truth means telling the whole truth. And that means summoning the courage to deliver bad news when necessary. And for some of us, especially those of us who are card-carrying people pleasers, telling the whole truth can be difficult indeed (especially if we're pretty sure that the truth will make somebody mad). Still, if we wish to fashion successful lives, we've got to learn to be totally truthful—part-time truth-telling doesn't cut the mustard.

Sometimes, honesty is difficult; sometimes, honesty is painful; sometimes, honesty is inconvenient; but honesty is always God's way. In the Book of Proverbs, we read, "The Lord detests lying lips, but he delights in men who are truthful" (12:22 NIV). Clearly, truth is God's way, and it must be our way, too, even when telling the truth is difficult.

God never called us to naïveté. He called us to integrity . . . . The biblical concept of integrity emphasizes mature innocence not childlike ignorance.

Beth Moore

Integrity of heart is indispensable.

John Calvin

Our life pursuits will reflect our character and personal integrity.

Franklin Graham

SOMETHING TO THINK ABOUT

One of your greatest possessions is integrity . . . don't lose it. Billy Graham was right when he said: "Integrity is the glue that holds our way of life together. We must constantly strive to keep our integrity intact. When wealth is lost, nothing is lost; when health is lost, something is lost; when character is lost, all is lost."

Devotion #67

FOCUSING ON GOD

Let us lay aside every weight and the sin that so easily ensnares us, and run with endurance the race that lies before us, keeping our eyes on Jesus, the source and perfecter of our faith.
Hebrews 12:1-2 HCSB

Now that your diploma is signed, sealed, and securely hung on the wall, it's time for the next leg of your life's journey. This day, like every other, is filled to the brim with opportunities, challenges, and choices. But, no choice that you make is more important than the choice you make concerning God. Today, you will either place Him at the center of your life—or not—and the consequences of that choice have implications that are both temporal and eternal.

Sometimes, we don't intentionally neglect God; we simply allow ourselves to become overwhelmed with the demands of daily life. And then, without our even realizing it, we gradually drift away from the One we need most. Thankfully, God never drifts away from us. He remains always present, always steadfast, always loving.

As you begin this day, place God and His Son where they belong: in your head, in your prayers, on your lips, and in your heart. And then, with God as your guide and companion, let the journey begin . . .

MORE FROM GOD'S WORD ABOUT FOCUSING ON JESUS

"Follow Me," Jesus told them, "and I will make you into fishers of men!" Immediately they left their nets and followed Him..

Mark 1:17-18 HCSB

You did not choose Me, but I chose you. I appointed you that you should go out and produce fruit, and that your fruit should remain, so that whatever you ask the Father in My name, He will give you.

John 15:16 HCSB

Then He said to them all, "If anyone wants to come with Me, he must deny himself, take up his cross daily, and follow Me."

Luke 9:23 HCSB

I, therefore, the prisoner in the Lord, urge you to walk worthy of the calling you have received.

Ephesians 4:1 HCSB

For those whose lives are according to the flesh think about the things of the flesh, but those whose lives are according to the Spirit, about the things of the Spirit.

Romans 8:5 HCSB

Jesus challenges you and me to keep our focus daily
on the cross of His will if we want
to be His disciples.

Anne Graham Lotz

It is important to set goals because if you do not
have a plan, a goal, a direction, a purpose,
and a focus, you are not going to accomplish
anything for the glory of God.

Bill Bright

Jesus makes God visible.
But that truth does not make Him somehow less
than God. He is equally supreme with God.

Anne Graham Lotz

Jesus was the perfect reflection of God's nature
in every situation He encountered
during His time here on earth.

Bill Hybels

SOMETHING TO THINK ABOUT

How much time do you spend focusing on God and His will for your life? If you answered, "Not much," it's time to reorder your priorities.

Devotion #68

DO FIRST THINGS FIRST

Therefore, get your minds ready for action, being self-disciplined . . . .
1 Peter 1:13 HCSB

First things first. These words are easy to speak but hard to put into practice. For busy people living in a demanding world, placing first things first can be difficult indeed. Why? Because so many people are expecting so many things from us!

If you're having trouble prioritizing your day, perhaps you've been trying to organize your life according to your own plans, not God's. A better strategy, of course, is to take your daily obligations and place them in the hands of the One who created you. To do so, you must prioritize your day according to God's commandments, and you must seek His will and His wisdom in all matters. Then, you can face the day with the assurance that the same God who created our universe out of nothingness will help you place first things first in your own life.

Do you feel overwhelmed or confused? Turn the concerns of this day over to God—prayerfully, earnestly, and often. Then, listen for His answer . . . and trust the answer He gives.

So teach us to number our days,
that we may gain a heart of wisdom.
Psalm 90:12 NKJV

Great relief and satisfaction can come from seeking God's priorities for us in each season, discerning what is "best" in the midst of many noble opportunities, and pouring our most excellent energies into those things.
Beth Moore

Not now becomes never.
Martin Luther

I've found that the worst thing I can do when it comes to any kind of potential pressure situation is to put off dealing with it.
John Maxwell

SOMETHING TO THINK ABOUT

Do first things first, and keep your focus on high-priority tasks. And remember this: your highest priority should be your relationship with God and His Son.

Devotion #69

SHARING YOUR TESTIMONY

This and this only has been my appointed work:
getting this news to those who have never heard of God,
and explaining how it works
by simple faith and plain truth.
1 Timothy 2:7 MSG

A good way to build your faith is by talking about it—and that's precisely what God wants you to do.

In his second letter to Timothy, Paul shares a message to believers of every generation when he writes, "God has not given us a spirit of timidity" (1:7). Paul's meaning is clear: When sharing your testimony, you must be courageous and unashamed.

Let's face facts: You live in a world that desperately needs the healing message of Jesus Christ. Every believer, including you, bears responsibility for sharing the Good News. And it is important to remember that you give your testimony through your words and your actions.

So today, preach the Gospel through your words and your deeds . . . but not necessarily in that order.

Whatever I tell you in the dark, speak in the light;
and what you hear in the ear, preach on the housetops.
Matthew 10:27 NKJV

If we are ever going to be or do anything
for our Lord, now is the time.
Vance Havner

One of the best ways to witness to family,
friends, and neighbors is to let them see
the difference Jesus has made in your life.
Anne Graham Lotz

Being an effective witness means that
we call attention to our testimony
and leave the results to Him.
Calvin Miller

SOMETHING TO THINK ABOUT

Your story is important. D. L. Moody, the famed evangelist from Chicago, said, "Remember, a small light will do a great deal when it is in a very dark place. Put one little tallow candle in the middle of a large hall, and it will give a great deal of light." Make certain that your candle is always lit. Give your testimony, and trust God to do the rest.

Devotion #70

FINDING COURAGE FOR YOUR JOURNEY

Be strong and courageous, and do the work.
Don't be afraid or discouraged,
for the Lord God, my God, is with you.
He won't leave you or forsake you.
1 Chronicles 28:20 HCSB

Because we are saved by a risen Christ, we can have hope for the future, no matter how desperate our circumstances may seem. After all, God has promised that we are His throughout eternity. And, He has told us that we must place our hopes in Him.

Today, as you make plans to begin the next phase of your journey, summon the courage to follow God. Even if the path seems difficult, even if your heart is fearful, trust your Heavenly Father and follow Him. Trust Him with your day and your life. Do His work, care for His children, and share His Good News. Let Him guide your steps. He will not lead you astray.

MORE FROM GOD'S WORD ABOUT GOD'S GUIDANCE

In all your ways acknowledge Him,
and He shall direct your paths.
Proverbs 3:6 NKJV

Yet Lord, You are our Father; we are the clay,
and You are our potter;
we all are the work of Your hands.
Isaiah 64:8 HCSB

Lord, You are my lamp;
the Lord illuminates my darkness.
2 Samuel 22:29 HCSB

Every morning he wakes me.
He teaches me to listen like a student.
The Lord God helps me learn . . . .
Isaiah 50:4-5 NCV

Teach me Your way, Lord, and I will live by Your truth.
Give me an undivided mind to fear Your name.
Psalm 86:11 HCSB

Down through the centuries, in times of trouble and trial, God has brought courage to the hearts of those who love Him. The Bible is filled with assurances of God's help and comfort in every kind of trouble which might cause fears to arise in the human heart. You can look ahead with promise, hope, and joy.

Billy Graham

Choose Jesus Christ! Deny yourself, take up the Cross, and follow Him—for the world must be shown. The world must see, in us, a discernible, visible, startling difference.

Elisabeth Elliot

The Christian faith engages the profoundest problems the human mind can entertain and solves them completely and simply by pointing to the Lamb of God.

A. W. Tozer

SOMETHING TO THINK ABOUT

God has a plan for your life. Your job is to discover that plan and follow it.

Devotion #71

JUDGE NOT

Do not judge, and you will not be judged.
Do not condemn, and you will not be condemned.
Forgive, and you will be forgiven.
Luke 6:37 HCSB

Here's something worth thinking about: If you judge other people harshly, God will judge you in the same fashion. But that's not all (thank goodness!). The Bible also promises that if you forgive others, you, too, will be forgiven. Have you developed the bad habit of behaving yourself like an amateur judge and jury, assigning blame and condemnation wherever you go? If so, it's time to grow up and obey God. When it comes to judging everything and everybody, God doesn't need your help . . . and He doesn't want it.

Speak and act as those who will be judged
by the law of freedom. For judgment is without mercy
to the one who hasn't shown mercy.
Mercy triumphs over judgment.
James 2:12-13 HCSB

Therefore, whatever you want others to do for you,
do also the same for them—
this is the Law and the Prophets.
Matthew 7:12 HCSB

Christians think they are prosecuting attorneys or judges, when, in reality, God has called all of us to be witnesses.
Warren Wiersbe

It is time that the followers of Jesus revise their language and learn to speak respectfully of non-Christian peoples.
Lottie Moon

Jesus lives in the community;
He only visits the church.
Anonymous

SOMETHING TO THINK ABOUT

When you catch yourself being overly judgmental, try to stop yourself and interrupt your critical thoughts before you become angry.

Devotion #72

KNOWING WHEN TO SAY NO

Do not be conquered by evil,
but conquer evil with good.
Romans 12:21 HCSB

Sometimes, you may feel pressured to compromise yourself, and you may be afraid of what will happen if you firmly say "No." You may be afraid that you'll be rejected. But here's a tip: don't worry too much about rejection, especially when you're rejected for doing the right thing.

Pleasing other people is a good thing . . . up to a point. But you must never allow your "willingness to please" to interfere with your own good judgement or with God's commandments.

Instead of being afraid of rejection, focus on pleasing your Creator first and always. And when it comes to the world and all its inhabitants, don't worry too much about the folks you can't please. Focus, instead, on doing the right thing—and leave the rest up to God.

He replied, "Every plant that My heavenly Father didn't plant will be uprooted."
Matthew 15:13 HCSB

Too many Christians have geared their program to please, to entertain, and to gain favor from this world. We are concerned with how much, instead of how little, like this age we can become.
Billy Graham

Those who follow the crowd usually get lost in it.
Rick Warren

You must never sacrifice your relationship with God for the sake of a relationship with another person.
Charles Stanley

SOMETHING TO THINK ABOUT

Maturity means that you make wise choices. Immaturity means that you continue making unwise choices . . . it's as simple as that.

Devotion #73

BEYOND BUSYNESS

Be careful not to forget the Lord.
Deuteronomy 6:12 HCSB

Each day has 1,440 minutes—do you value your relationship with God enough to spend a few of those minutes with Him? He deserves that much of your time and more. But if you find that you're simply "too busy" for a daily chat with your Father in heaven, it's time to take a long, hard look at your priorities and your values.

If you've acquired the unfortunate habit of trying to "squeeze" God into the corners of your life, it's time to reshuffle the items on your to-do list by placing God first. God wants your undivided attention, not the leftovers of your day. So, if you haven't already done so, form the habit of spending quality time with your Creator. He deserves it . . . and so, for that matter, do you.

MORE FROM GOD'S WORD ABOUT YOUR PRIORITIES

Don't abandon wisdom, and she will watch over you; love her, and she will guard you.
Proverbs 4:6 HCSB

And I pray this: that your love will keep on growing in knowledge and every kind of discernment, so that you can determine what really matters and can be pure and blameless in the day of Christ.
Philippians 1:9 HCSB

So teach us to number our days, that we may gain a heart of wisdom.
Psalm 90:12 NKJV

For where your treasure is, there your heart will be also.
Luke 12:34 HCSB

He said to them all, "If anyone desires to come after Me, let him deny himself, and take up his cross daily, and follow Me. For whoever desires to save his life will lose it, but whoever loses his life for My sake will save it."
Luke 9:23-24 NKJV

You're busy with all the pressures of the world around you, but in that busyness you're missing the most important element of all—God's ongoing presence that is available to you.

Bill Hybels

Are you weak? Weary? Confused? Troubled? Pressured? How is your relationship with God? Is it held in its place of priority? I believe the greater the pressure, the greater your need for time alone with Him.

Kay Arthur

The foe of opportunity is preoccupation. Just when God sends along a chance to turn a great victory for mankind, some of us are too busy puttering around to notice it.

A. W. Tozer

SOMETHING TO THINK ABOUT

Decide how much of your time God deserves, and then give it to Him. Don't organize your day so that God gets "what's left." Give Him what you honestly believe He deserves.

Devotion #74

FINDING POSITIVE FRIENDS

Iron sharpens iron,
and one man sharpens another.
Proverbs 27:17 HCSB

When you associate with positive people, you will feel better about yourself and your world—when you hang out with negative people, you won't. So here's the question: do you want to feel better about yourself and your circumstances . . . or not? The answer you give should help you determine the friends you choose to make—and keep.

If you're really serious about being an optimistic, upbeat, hope-filled Christian, make sure that your friends feel the same way. Because if you choose to hang out with upbeat people, you'll tend to be an upbeat person, too. But if you hang out with the critics, the cynics, and the naysayers, you'll find yourself become a cynic, too. And life is far too short for that.

MORE FROM GOD'S WORD ABOUT FRIENDS

Beloved, if God so loved us,
we also ought to love one another.
1 John 4:11 NKJV

A friend loves at all times,
and a brother is born for a difficult time.
Proverbs 17:17 HCSB

Finally, all of you be of one mind,
having compassion for one another;
love as brothers, be tenderhearted, be courteous.
1 Peter 3:8 NKJV

The one who loves his brother remains in the light,
and there is no cause for stumbling in him.
1 John 2:10 HCSB

No one has greater love than this, that someone would
lay down his life for his friends.
John 15:13 HCSB

The next best thing to being wise oneself is
to live in a circle of those who are.
C. S. Lewis

Though I know intellectually how vulnerable
I am to pride and power, I am the last one to know
when I succumb to their seduction.
That's why spiritual Lone Rangers are
so dangerous—and why we must depend on
trusted brothers and sisters who love us
enough to tell us the truth.
Chuck Colson

If you choose to awaken a passion for God,
you will have to choose your friends wisely.
Lisa Bevere

Insomuch as anyone pushes you nearer to God,
he or she is your friend.
Anonymous

SOMETHING TO THINK ABOUT

You'll probably end up behaving like your friends behave . . . and if that's a scary thought, it time to make a new set of friends.

Devotion #75

BE PATIENT AND TRUST GOD

Trust in Him at all times, you people;
pour out your heart before Him;
God is a refuge for us.
Psalm 62:8 NKJV

As individuals, as families, and as a nation, we are impatient for the changes that we so earnestly desire. We want solutions to our problems, and we want them right now! But sometimes, life's greatest challenges defy easy solutions, so we must be patient.

Psalm 37:7 commands us to "Rest in the Lord, and wait patiently for Him" (NKJV). But for most of us, waiting quietly for God is difficult. Why? Because we are imperfect beings who seek solutions to our problems today, if not sooner. We seek to manage our lives according to our own timetables, not God's. To do so is a mistake. Instead of impatiently tapping our fingers, we should fold our fingers and pray. When we do, our Heavenly Father will reward us in His own miraculous way and in His own perfect time.

He said to them, "It is not for you to know times or periods that the Father has set by His own authority."
Acts 1:7 HCSB

Be patient. God is using today's difficulties to strengthen you for tomorrow.
He is equipping you. The God who makes things grow will help you bear fruit.
Max Lucado

God has a designated time when his promise will be fulfilled and the prayer will be answered.
Jim Cymbala

There is no place for faith if we expect God to fulfill immediately what he promises.
John Calvin

SOMETHING TO THINK ABOUT

Want other people to be patient with you? Then you must do the same for them. Never expect other people to be more patient with you than you are with them.

Devotion #76

SEEING THINGS FROM GOD'S PERSPECTIVE

All I'm doing right now, friends, is showing how these things pertain to Apollos and me so that you will learn restraint and not rush into making judgments without knowing all the facts. It is important to look at things from God's point of view. I would rather not see you inflating or deflating reputations based on mere hearsay.
1 Corinthians 4:6 MSG

Sometimes, amid the demands of daily life, we lose perspective. Life seems out of balance, and the pressures of everyday living seem overwhelming. What's needed is a fresh perspective, a restored sense of balance . . . and God. If we call upon the Lord and seek to see the world through His eyes, He will give us guidance and wisdom and perspective.

When we make God's priorities our priorities, He will lead us according to His plan and according to His commandments. God's reality is the ultimate reality. May we live accordingly.

Yet Lord, You are our Father; we are the clay,
and You are our potter;
we all are the work of Your hands.
Isaiah 64:8 HCSB

Like a shadow declining swiftly . . . away . . .
like the dew of the morning gone with the heat of
the day; like the wind in the treetops,
like a wave of the sea, so are our lives on earth
when seen in light of eternity.
Ruth Bell Graham

The Bible is a remarkable commentary on
perspective. Through its divine message, we are
brought face to face with issues and tests in daily
living and how, by the power of the Holy Spirit,
we are enabled to respond positively to them.
Luci Swindoll

SOMETHING TO THINK ABOUT

God has a wonderful plan for your life. And the time to start looking for that plan—and living it—is now. Discovering God's plan begins with prayer, but it doesn't end there. You've also got to work at it.

Devotion #77

DECIDING TO PLEASE GOD

For am I now trying to win the favor of people, or God?
Or am I striving to please people?
If I were still trying to please people,
I would not be a slave of Christ.
Galatians 1:10 HCSB

Sometimes, it's very tempting to be a people-pleaser. But usually, it's the wrong thing to do.

When you worry too much about pleasing dates or friends, you may not worry enough about pleasing God—and when you fail to please God, you inevitably pay a very high price for your mistaken priorities.

Whom will you try to please today: God or your friends? Your obligation is most certainly not to your peers or to your date. Your obligation is to an all-knowing and perfect God. Trust Him always. Love Him always. Praise Him always. And seek to please Him and only Him. Always.

Therefore, whether we are at home or away,
we make it our aim to be pleasing to Him.
2 Corinthians 5:9 HCSB

People who constantly, and fervently, seek
the approval of others live with an identity crisis.
They don't know who they are,
and they are defined by what others think of them.
Charles Stanley

Make God's will the focus of your life day by day.
If you seek to please Him and Him alone,
you'll find yourself satisfied with life.
Kay Arthur

Every day, I find countless opportunities to decide
whether I will obey God and demonstrate my love
for Him or try to please myself or the world system.
God is waiting for my choices.
Bill Bright

SOMETHING TO THINK ABOUT

If you are burdened with a "people-pleasing" personality, outgrow it. Realize that you can't please all of the people all of the time (including your dates), nor should you attempt to.

Devotion #78

EXPERIENCING SILENCE

Be still, and know that I am God.
Psalm 46:10 NKJV

Here's a simple little prescription for character-building: carve out a little time for silence every day.

Here in our noisy world, silence is highly underrated. Many of us can't even seem to walk from the front door to the street without a cell phone or an iPod in our ear. The world seems to grow louder day by day, and our senses seem to be invaded at every turn. But, if we allow the distractions of a clamorous society to separate us from God's peace, we do ourselves a profound disservice. So if we're wise, we make time each day for quiet reflection. And when we do, we are rewarded.

Do you take time each day for an extended period of silence? And during those precious moments, do you sincerely open your heart to your Creator? If so, you will be blessed. If not, then the struggles and stresses of everyday living may rob you of the peace that should rightfully be yours because of your personal relationship with Christ. So take time each day to quietly commune with your Creator. When you do, those moments of silence will enable you to participate more fully in the only source of peace that endures: God's peace.

MORE FROM GOD'S WORD ABOUT SILENCE

Be silent before the Lord and wait expectantly for Him.
Psalm 37:7 HCSB

In quietness and confidence shall be your strength.
Isaiah 30:15 NKJV

I wait quietly before God,
for my salvation comes from him.
Psalm 62:1 NLT

The one who is from God listens to God's words.
This is why you don't listen,
because you are not from God.
John 8:47 HCSB

Listen in silence before me . . . .
Isaiah 41:1 NLT

Instead of waiting for the feeling, wait upon God. You can do this by growing still and quiet, then expressing in prayer what your mind knows is true about Him, even if your heart doesn't feel it at this moment.

Shirley Dobson

There are times when to speak is to violate the moment—when silence represents the highest respect. The word for such times is reverence.

Max Lucado

I have come to recognize that He never asks us to do anything He has not already done. He never takes us anyplace where He has not been ahead of us. What He is after is not performance, but a relationship with us.

Gloria Gaither

SOMETHING TO THINK ABOUT

Want to talk to God? Then don't make Him shout. If you really want to hear from God, go to a quiet place and listen. If you keep listening long enough and carefully enough, He'll start talking.

Devotion #79

THE CHOICE TO BE JOYFUL

Rejoice in the Lord always.
I will say it again: Rejoice!
Philippians 4:4 HCSB

You can't really get to know God until you genuinely experience God's joy for yourself. It's not enough to hear somebody else talk about being a joyful Christian—you must experience Christ's joy in order to understand it. Does that mean that you'll be a joy-filled believer 24 hours a day, seven days a week, from this moment on? Nope. But it does mean that you can experience God's joy personally, frequently, intensely.

So here's a prescription for better spiritual health: Open the door of your soul to Christ. When you do, He will give you peace and joy . . . heaping helpings of peace and joy.

Make me hear joy and gladness.
Psalm 51:8 NKJV

The good life—the one that truly satisfies—
exists only when we stop wanting a better one.
Charles Swindoll

Rejoice, the Lord is King; Your Lord
and King adore! Rejoice, give thanks
and sing and triumph evermore.
Charles Wesley

We all go through pain and sorrow,
but the presence of God, like a warm,
comforting blanket, can shield us and protect us,
and allow the deep inner joy to surface,
even in the most devastating circumstances.
Barbara Johnson

SOMETHING TO THINK ABOUT

Joy begins with a choice: the choice to establish a genuine relationship with God and His Son. As Amy Carmichael correctly observed, "Joy is not gush; joy is not mere jolliness. Joy is perfect acquiescence, acceptance, and rest in God's will, whatever comes."

Devotion #80

LEARNING GOD'S LESSONS SOONER RATHER THAN LATER

Incline your ear to wisdom,
and apply your heart to understanding.
Proverbs 2:2 NKJV

One way that we learn about God is by learning the lessons that He is trying so desperately to teach us. But when it comes to learning God's lessons, most of us can be quite hardheaded. Why? Because we are, by nature, stubborn creatures; and because we seem destined, at times, to make things hard on ourselves.

As we go about the business of learning life's lessons, we can either do things the easy way or the hard way. The easy way can be summed up as follows: when God tries to teach us something, we learn it . . . the first time! Unfortunately, too many of us learn much more slowly than that.

When we resist God's instruction, He continues to teach, whether we like it or not. Our challenge, then, is to discern God's lessons from the experiences of everyday life. Hopefully, we learn those lessons sooner rather than later because the sooner we do so, the sooner He can move on to the next lesson and the next and the next . . .

Teach me to do Your will, for You are my God.
May Your gracious Spirit lead me on level ground.
Psalm 143:10 HCSB

The wise man gives proper appreciation in his life to his past. He learns to sift the sawdust of heritage in order to find the nuggets that make the current moment have any meaning.
Grady Nutt

The wonderful thing about God's schoolroom is that we get to grade our own papers. You see, He doesn't test us so He can learn how well we're doing. He tests us so we can discover how well we're doing.
Charles Swindoll

A big difference exists between a head full of knowledge and the words of God literally abiding in us.
Beth Moore

SOMETHING TO THINK ABOUT

Learning about God's truth is "head knowledge" and it is incomplete. Learning, doing, and experiencing God's truth is "head-and-heart knowledge" . . . and it is complete.

Devotion #81

THE REWARDS OF DISCIPLINE

The one who follows instruction is on the path to life,
but the one who rejects correction goes astray.
Proverbs 10:17 HCSB

Students everywhere understand the profound sense of joy that accompanies two little words: "School's out!" In a brief, two-word exclamatory sentence, so much is said. "School's out!" means no more homework, no more papers, no more grades, and no more standardized tests. "School's out!" means it's time for a much-needed break from the daily grind. "School's out!" means it's time to put the books—and the worries—away. But before the celebration gets out of hand, be forewarned: "School's out!" does not mean that our work is done. To the contrary, the real work is probably just beginning.

Those who study the Bible are confronted again and again with God's intention that His children lead disciplined lives. God doesn't reward laziness. To the contrary, He expects believers to adopt a disciplined approach to their lives. In Proverbs 28:19, the message is clear: work diligently and consistently, and then expect a bountiful harvest. But never expect the harvest to precede the labor.

As a recent graduate, you've earned the right to proclaim "School's out!" at the top of your lungs. And then, when all the shouting is over, remember that God rewards discipline just as certainly as He punishes indolence. And if you're not sure what the word *indolence* means, then school isn't really out yet, now is it? Your dictionary is in that stack of books over there in the corner. Happy reading!

MORE FROM GOD'S WORD ABOUT DISCIPLINE

No discipline seems enjoyable at the time, but painful. Later on, however, it yields the fruit of peace and righteousness to those who have been trained by it.
Hebrews 12:11 HCSB

I discipline my body and bring it under strict control, so that after preaching to others, I myself will not be disqualified.
1 Corinthians 9:27 HCSB

Therefore by their fruits you will know them.
Matthew 7:20 NKJV

Even a young man is known by his actions—
by whether his behavior is pure and upright.
Proverbs 20:11 HCSB

If one examines the secret behind a championship
football team, a magnificent orchestra,
or a successful business,
the principal ingredient is invariably discipline.
James Dobson

What our Lord said about cross-bearing and
obedience is not in fine type.
It is in bold print on the face of the contract.
Vance Havner

Work is doing it. Discipline is doing it every day.
Diligence is doing it well every day.
Dave Ramsey

SOMETHING TO THINK ABOUT

If you're a disciplined person, you'll earn big rewards. If you're undisciplined, you won't.

Devotion #82

FOLLOWING THE GOLDEN RULE

Therefore, whatever you want others to do for you,
do also the same for them—
this is the Law and the Prophets.
Matthew 7:12 HCSB

The words of Matthew 7:12 remind us that, as believers in Christ, we are commanded to treat others as we wish to be treated. This commandment is, indeed, the Golden Rule for Christians of every generation.

Kindness is a choice. It's the choice to observe the Golden Rule "in everything." God intends that we make the conscious choice to treat others with kindness and respect, no matter our circumstances, no matter our emotions. Kindness, therefore, is a choice that we, as Christians must make many times each day.

When we weave the thread of kindness into the very fabric of our lives, we give a priceless gift to others, and we give glory to the One who gave His life for us. As believers, we must do no less.

Just as you want others to do for you,
do the same for them.
Luke 6:31 HCSB

Do all the good you can. By all the means you can. In all the ways you can. In all the places you can. At all the times you can. To all the people you can. As long as ever you can.
John Wesley

The Golden Rule starts at home, but it should never stop there.
Marie T. Freeman

If we have the true love of God in our hearts, we will show it in our lives. We will not have to go up and down the earth proclaiming it. We will show it in everything we say or do.
D. L. Moody

SOMETHING TO THINK ABOUT

How would you feel? When you're trying to decide how to treat another person, ask yourself this question: "How would I feel if somebody treated me that way?" Then, treat the other person the way that you would want to be treated.

Devotion #83

TRUSTING GOD'S WORD

For the word of God is living and effective and sharper than any two-edged sword, penetrating as far as to divide soul, spirit, joints, and marrow; it is a judge of the ideas and thoughts of the heart.
Hebrews 4:12 HCSB

God's Word is unlike any other book. The words of Matthew 4:4 remind us that, "Man shall not live by bread alone but by every word that proceedeth out of the mouth of God" (KJV). As believers, we are instructed to study the Bible and meditate upon its meaning for our lives, yet far too many Bibles are laid aside by well-intentioned believers who would like to study the Bible if they could "just find the time."

Warren Wiersbe observed, "When the child of God looks into the Word of God, he sees the Son of God. And, he is transformed by the Spirit of God to share in the glory of God." Enough said.

Heaven and earth will pass away,
but My words will never pass away.
Matthew 24:35 HCSB

Faith is the virtue that enables us to believe and obey the Word of God, for faith comes from hearing and hearing from the Word of God.
Franklin Graham

Weave the unveiling fabric of God's word through your heart and mind. It will hold strong, even if the rest of life unravels.
Gigi Graham Tchividjian

Meditating upon His Word will inevitably bring peace of mind, strength of purpose, and power for living.
Bill Bright

SOMETHING TO THINK ABOUT

If you have a choice to make, the Bible can help you make it. If you've got questions, the Bible has answers.

Devotion #84

LEARNING TO WORRY LESS

Therefore don't worry about tomorrow,
because tomorrow will worry about itself.
Each day has enough trouble of its own.
Matthew 6:34 HCSB

Because life is sometimes difficult, and because we have understandable fears about the uncertainty of the future, we worry. At times, we may find ourselves fretting over the countless details of everyday life. We may worry about our relationships, our finances, our health, or any number of potential problems, some large and some small.

If you're a "worrier" by nature, it's probably time to rethink the way that you think! Perhaps you've formed the unfortunate habit of focusing too intently on the negative aspects of life while spending too little time counting your blessings. If so, take your worries to God . . . and leave them there. When you do, you'll learn to worry a little less and to trust God a little more—and that's as it should be because God is trustworthy, you are protected, and your future can be intensely bright.

MORE FROM GOD'S WORD ABOUT WORRY

Don't worry about anything, but in everything, through prayer and petition with thanksgiving, let your requests be made known to God.
Philippians 4:6 HCSB

Therefore don't worry about tomorrow, because tomorrow will worry about itself. Each day has enough trouble of its own.
Matthew 6:34 HCSB

Yea, though I walk through the valley of the shadow of death, I will fear no evil: for thou art with me; thy rod and thy staff they comfort me.
Psalm 23:4 KJV

I will be with you when you pass through the waters . . . when you walk through the fire . . . the flame will not burn you. For I the Lord your God, the Holy One of Israel, and your Savior.
Isaiah 43:2-3 HCSB

Those who trust in the Lord are like Mount Zion. It cannot be shaken; it remains forever.
Psalm 125:1 HCSB

Our fears for today, our worries about tomorrow,
and even the powers of hell
can't keep God's love away.
Bill Bright

The busier we are, the easier it is to worry,
the greater the temptation to worry,
the greater the need to be alone with God.
Charles Stanley

God may say "Wait," but He never says, "Worry."
Anonymous

Today is mine. Tomorrow is none of my business.
If I peer anxiously into the fog of the future,
I will strain my spiritual eyes so that
I will not see clearly what is required of me now.
Elisabeth Elliott

SOMETHING TO THINK ABOUT

Keep life in perspective: Your life is an integral part of God's grand plan, so don't become unduly upset over the minor inconveniences of life, and don't worry too much about today's setbacks—they're temporary.

Devotion #85

CHOOSING TO BE GENEROUS

Each person should do as he has decided in his heart—
not out of regret or out of necessity,
for God loves a cheerful giver.
2 Corinthians 9:7 HCSB

Are you a cheerful giver? If you intend to obey God's commandments, you must be. When you give, God looks not only at the quality of your gift, but also at the condition of your heart. If you give generously, joyfully, and without complaint, you obey God's Word. But, if you make your gifts grudgingly, or if the motivation for your gift is selfish, you disobey your Creator, even if you have tithed in accordance with Biblical principles.

Today, take God's commandments to heart and make this pledge: Be a cheerful, generous, courageous giver. The world needs your help, and you need the spiritual rewards that will be yours when you give faithfully, prayerfully, and cheerfully.

Bear one another's burdens,
and so fulfill the law of Christ.
Galatians 6:2 NKJV

Two works of mercy set a man free:
forgive and you will be forgiven,
and give and you will receive.
St. Augustine

Let us give according to our incomes,
lest God make our incomes match our gifts.
Peter Marshall

What is your focus today?
Joy comes when it is Jesus first,
others second . . . then you.
Kay Arthur

SOMETHING TO THINK ABOUT

There is a direct relationship between generosity and joy—the more you give to others, the more joy you will experience for yourself.

Devotion #86

ON THE ROAD AHEAD, PLACE HOLINESS BEFORE HAPPINESS

Blessed are those who hunger
and thirst for righteousness,
because they will be filled.
Matthew 5:6 HCSB

Because you are an imperfect human being, you are not "perfectly" happy—and that's perfectly okay with God. He is far less concerned with your happiness than He is with your holiness.

God continuously reveals Himself in everyday life, but He does not do so in order to make you contented; He does so in order to lead you to His Son. So don't be overly concerned with your current level of happiness: it will change. Be more concerned with the current state of your relationship with Christ: He does not change. And because your Savior transcends time and space, you can be comforted in the knowledge that in the end, His joy will become your joy . . . for all eternity.

MORE FROM GOD'S WORD ABOUT HOLINESS

Real wisdom, God's wisdom, begins with a holy life and is characterized by getting along with others. It is gentle and reasonable, overflowing with mercy and blessings, not hot one day and cold the next, not two-faced.
James 3:17 MSG

Pursue peace with all people, and holiness, without which no one will see the Lord:
Hebrews 12:14 NKJV

Since everything here today might well be gone tomorrow, do you see how essential it is to live a holy life?
2 Peter 3:11 MSG

Because the eyes of the Lord are on the righteous and His ears are open to their request. But the face of the Lord is against those who do evil.
1 Peter 3:12 HCSB

Therefore, come out from among them and be separate, says the Lord; do not touch any unclean thing, and I will welcome you.
2 Corinthians 6:17 HCSB

Holiness isn't in a style of dress. It's not a matter of rules and regulations. It's a way of life that emanates quietness and rest, joy in family, shared pleasures with friends, the help of a neighbor—
and the hope of a Savior.

Joni Eareckson Tada

Believers are in the world, and yet they must not be absorbed by it. If Christians are to fulfill their purposes in the world, they must not be chilled by the indifferent, godless society in which they live.

Billy Graham

There is no detour to holiness. Jesus came to the resurrection through the cross, not around it.

Leighton Ford

SOMETHING TO THINK ABOUT

God is holy and wants you to be holy. Christ died to make you holy. Make sure that your response to Christ's sacrifice is worthy of Him.

Devotion #87

WHAT DOESN'T CHANGE

I the Lord do not change.
Malachi 3:6 HCSB

Graduation is a time of transition. Everything around you may seem to be in a state of flux, and you may be required to make lots of adjustments. If all these events have left your head spinning and your heart pounding, don't worry: although the world is in a state of constant change, God is not.

Even if the changes in your life are unfolding at a furious pace, you can be comforted in the knowledge that your Heavenly Father is the rock that cannot be shaken.

As a recent graduate, you're facing an exciting time, a time filled with possibilities and opportunities. But, if your transition to the next phase of life proves difficult, don't worry: God is far bigger than any challenge you may face.

Remember that "Jesus Christ is the same yesterday, today, and forever" (Hebrews 13:8 NKJV). And rest assured: It is precisely because your Savior does not change that you can face the transitions of life with courage for today and hope for tomorrow.

MORE FROM GOD'S WORD ABOUT CHANGE

The sensible see danger and take cover;
the foolish keep going and are punished.
Proverbs 27:12 HCSB

But may the God of all grace, who called us
to His eternal glory by Christ Jesus,
after you have suffered a while, perfect, establish,
strengthen, and settle you.
1 Peter 5:10 NKJV

Therefore we do not lose heart.
Even though our outward man is perishing,
yet the inward man is being renewed day by day.
2 Corinthians 4:16 NKJV

Create in me a clean heart, O God,
and renew a steadfast spirit within me.
Psalm 51:10 NKJV

Finally, brothers, rejoice. Be restored, be encouraged,
be of the same mind, be at peace,
and the God of love and peace will be with you.
2 Corinthians 13:11 HCSB

The secret of contentment in the midst of change is found in having roots in the changeless Christ— the same yesterday, today and forever.

Ed Young

The resurrection of Jesus Christ is the power of God to change history and to change lives.

Bill Bright

Conditions are always changing; therefore, I must not be dependent upon conditions. What matters supremely is my soul and my relationship to God.

Corrie ten Boom

SOMETHING TO THINK ABOUT

The world continues to change, as do you. Change is inevitable—you can either roll with it or be rolled over by it. In order to avoid the latter, you should choose the former . . . and trust God as you go.

Devotion #88

CHOOSING TO AVOID THE CONSTANT CRITICS

Therefore encourage one another
and build each other up
as you are already doing.
1 Thessalonians 5:11 HCSB

If you want to feel better about yourself, find friends who are willing to offer you a steady stream of encouragement. And while you're at it, steer clear of the ceaseless critics and the chronic fault-finders.

In the book of James, we are issued a clear warning: "Don't criticize one another, brothers" (4:11 HCSB). Undoubtedly, James understood the paralyzing power of chronic negativity, and so should you.

Negativity is highly contagious, and can be highly hazardous to your sense of self-worth. So do yourself a major-league favor: find friends who make you feel better about yourself, not worse. Make no mistake: You deserve friends like that . . . and they deserve to have an encouraging friend like you.

Anxiety in a man's heart weighs it down,
but a good word cheers it up.
Proverbs 12:25 HCSB

It is helpful to remember the distinction between appreciation and affirmation. We appreciate what a person does, but we affirm who a person is.
Charles Swindoll

Never be afraid of the world's censure;
it's praise is much more to be dreaded.
C. H. Spurgeon

The scrutiny we give other people
should be for ourselves.
Oswald Chambers

SOMETHING TO THINK ABOUT

Think carefully about the things you say so that your words can be a "gift of encouragement" to others. Also, make sure to select friends who are a source of encouragement to you.

Devotion #89

YOUR STEWARDSHIP OF GOD'S GIFTS

I remind you to keep ablaze
the gift of God that is in you.
2 Timothy 1:6 HCSB

Do you want to be a faithful follower of Christ? Do you want to know God's will for your life? And do you trust God's promises? If so, then you will be a faithful steward of the gifts He has given you.

When you are a reliable steward of your talents, and when you give God that which is rightfully His, you experience the spiritual growth that always accompanies obedience to the Creator. But, if you attempt to shortchange God, either materially or spiritually, you will inevitably distance yourself from Him.

Everybody has special gifts, and you are no exception. Today, accept this challenge: value the talent that God has given you, nourish it, make it grow, and share it with the world. Manage your resources as if they were a one-of-a-kind treasure on loan from God, which, by the way, they are.

MORE FROM GOD'S WORD ABOUT YOUR GIFTS

Based on the gift they have received,
everyone should use it to serve others,
as good managers of the varied grace of God.
1 Peter 4:10 HCSB

Now there are different gifts, but the same Spirit.
There are different ministries, but the same Lord.
1 Corinthians 12:4-5 HCSB

Every generous act and every perfect gift is from above,
coming down from the Father of lights.
James 1:17 HCSB

According to the grace given to us, we have
different gifts: If prophecy, use it according to
the standard of faith; if service, in service;
if teaching, in teaching; if exhorting, in exhortation;
giving, with generosity; leading, with diligence;
showing mercy, with cheerfulness.
Romans 12:6-8 HCSB

Do not neglect the gift that is in you.
1 Timothy 4:14 HCSB

Natural abilities are like natural plants;
they need pruning by study.
Francis Bacon

One thing taught large in the Holy Scriptures is
that while God gives His gifts freely, He will require
a strict accounting of them at the end of the road.
Each man is personally responsible for his store,
be it large or small, and will be required to explain
his use of it before the judgment seat of Christ.
A. W. Tozer

All the blessings we enjoy are divine deposits,
committed to our trust on this condition:
that they should be dispensed for the benefit
of our neighbors.
John Calvin

SOMETHING TO THINK ABOUT

You have talents and opportunities which you can choose to use . . . or not. You must either use them or lose them.

Devotion #90

COURAGE FOR THE JOURNEY

Be alert, stand firm in the faith,
be brave and strong.
1 Corinthians 16:13 HCSB

A storm rose quickly on the Sea of Galilee, and the disciples were afraid. Although they had seen Jesus perform many miracles, the disciples feared for their lives, so they turned to their Savior, and He calmed the waters and the wind.

Sometimes, we, like the disciples, feel threatened by the inevitable storms of life. And when we are fearful, we, too, can turn to Christ for courage and for comfort.

From time to time, all of us, even the most devout believers, experience fear. But, as believers, we can live courageously in the promises of our Lord . . . and we should.

As you take the next step on your life's journey, you can be comforted: Wherever you find yourself, God is there. And, because He cares for you, you can live courageously.

MORE FROM GOD'S WORD ABOUT COURAGE

Be strong and courageous, and do the work.
Don't be afraid or discouraged, for the Lord God,
my God, is with you.
He won't leave you or forsake you.
1 Chronicles 28:20 HCSB

For God has not given us a spirit of fearfulness,
but one of power, love, and sound judgment.
2 Timothy 1:7 HCSB

Haven't I commanded you: be strong and courageous?
Do not be afraid or discouraged,
for the Lord your God is with you wherever you go.
Joshua 1:9 HCSB

But when Jesus heard it, He answered him,
"Don't be afraid. Only believe."
Luke 8:50 HCSB

But He said to them, "Why are you fearful,
you of little faith?" Then He got up and rebuked
the winds and the sea. And there was a great calm.
Matthew 8:26 HCSB

Faith not only can help you through a crisis,
it can help you to approach life after the hard times
with a whole new perspective.
It can help you adopt an outlook of hope and
courage through faith to face reality.

John Maxwell

Why rely on yourself and fall? Cast yourself upon
His arm. Be not afraid. He will not let you slip.
Cast yourself in confidence.
He will receive you and heal you.

St. Augustine

The truth of Christ brings assurance and so
removes the former problem of
fear and uncertainty.

A. W. Tozer

SOMETHING TO THINK ABOUT

With God as your partner, you have nothing to fear. Why? Because you and God, working together, can handle absolutely anything that comes your way. So the next time you'd like an extra measure of courage, recommit yourself to a true one-on-one relationship with your Creator. When you sincerely turn to Him, He will never fail you.

Devotion #91

AVOIDING THE TRAP OF PERFECTIONISM

Those who wait for perfect weather will never plant seeds; those who look at every cloud will never harvest crops . . . . Plant early in the morning, and work until evening, because you don't know if this or that will succeed. They might both do well.
Ecclesiastes 11:4,6 NCV

If you find yourself bound up by the chains of perfectionism, it's time to ask yourself who you're trying to impress, and why. If you're trying to impress other people, it's time to reconsider your priorities. Your first responsibility is to the Heavenly Father who created you and to His Son who saved you. Then, you bear a powerful responsibility to your family. But, when it comes to meeting society's unrealistic expectations, forget it!

Remember that when you accepted Christ as your Savior, God accepted you for all eternity. Now, it's your turn to accept yourself and your loved ones. When you do, you'll feel a tremendous weight being lifted from your shoulders. After all, pleasing God is simply a matter of obeying His commandments and accepting His Son. But as for pleasing everybody else? That's impossible!

The fear of human opinion disables;
trusting in God protects you from that.
Proverbs 29:25 MSG

The happiest people in the world are not those who have no problems, but the people who have learned to live with those things that are less than perfect.
James Dobson

What makes a Christian a Christian is not perfection but forgiveness.
Max Lucado

God is so inconceivably good.
He's not looking for perfection.
He already saw it in Christ.
He's looking for affection.
Beth Moore

SOMETHING TO THINK ABOUT

Don't let others define success for you. That's between you and God.

Devotion #92

THE DECISION TO CELEBRATE LIFE

This is the day the LORD has made;
we will rejoice and be glad in it.
Psalm 118:24 NKJV

The 118th Psalm reminds us that today, like every other day, is a cause for celebration. God gives us this day; He fills it to the brim with possibilities, and He challenges us to use it for His purposes. The day is presented to us fresh and clean at midnight, free of charge, but we must beware: Today is a non-renewable resource—once it's gone, it's gone forever. Our responsibility, of course, is to use this day in the service of God's will and according to His commandments.

Today, treasure the time that God has given you. Give Him the glory and the praise and the thanksgiving that He deserves. And search for the hidden possibilities that God has placed along your path. This day is a priceless gift from God, so use it joyfully and encourage others to do likewise. After all, this is the day the Lord has made.

MORE FROM GOD'S WORD ABOUT CELEBRATION

Rejoice in the Lord always.
I will say it again: Rejoice!
Philippians 4:4 HCSB

If they serve Him obediently,
they will end their days in prosperity
and their years in happiness.
Job 36:11 HCSB

The one who understands a matter finds success,
and the one who trusts in the Lord will be happy.
Proverbs 16:20 HCSB

A joyful heart is good medicine,
but a broken spirit dries up the bones.
Proverbs 17:22 HCSB

How happy is the man who does not follow
the advice of the wicked, or take the path of sinners,
or join a group of mockers!
Psalm 1:1 HCSB

If you can forgive the person you were,
accept the person you are, and believe in
the person you will become, you are headed for joy.
So celebrate your life.
Barbara Johnson

Some of us seem so anxious about avoiding hell
that we forget to celebrate
our journey toward heaven.
Philip Yancey

God has a course mapped out for your life,
and all the inadequacies in the world will not
change His mind. He will be with you every step of
the way. And though it may take time, He has
a celebration planned for when you cross over
the "Red Seas" of your life.
Charles Swindoll

SOMETHING TO THINK ABOUT

If you don't feel like celebrating, start counting your blessings. Before long, you'll realize that you have plenty of reasons to celebrate.

Devotion #93

ON THE ROAD AHEAD, CHOOSE TO TAKE WORSHIP SERIOUSLY

Happy are those who hear the joyful
call to worship, for they will walk in the light
of your presence, Lord.
Psalm 89:15 NLT

Do you take time each day to worship your Father in heaven, or do you wait until Sunday morning to praise Him for His blessings? The answer to this question will, in large part, determine the quality and direction of your spiritual life.

When we worship God every day of our lives, we are blessed. When we fail to worship God, for whatever reason, we forfeit the spiritual gifts that He intends for us.

Every day provides opportunities to put God where He belongs: at the center of our lives. When we do so, we worship Him not only with our words, but also with our deeds, and that's as it should be. For believers, God comes first. Always first.

MORE FROM GOD'S WORD ABOUT WORSHIP

But an hour is coming, and is now here, when the true worshipers will worship the Father in spirit and truth. Yes, the Father wants such people to worship Him. God is Spirit, and those who worship Him must worship in spirit and truth.

John 4:23-24 HCSB

So that at the name of Jesus every knee should bow—of those who are in heaven and on earth and under the earth—and every tongue should confess that Jesus Christ is Lord, to the glory of God the Father.

Philippians 2:10-11 HCSB

Worship the Lord your God and . . . serve Him only.

Matthew 4:10 HCSB

If anyone is thirsty, he should come to Me and drink!

John 7:37 HCSB

And every day they devoted themselves to meeting together in the temple complex, and broke bread from house to house. They ate their food with gladness and simplicity of heart, praising God and having favor with all the people. And every day the Lord added those being saved to them.

Acts 2:46-47 HCSB

We're here to be worshipers first and workers only second. The work done by a worshiper will have eternity in it.
A. W. Tozer

To worship Him in truth means to worship Him honestly, without hypocrisy, standing open and transparent before Him.
Anne Graham Lotz

Spiritual worship is focusing all we are on all He is.
Beth Moore

Worship is your spirit responding to God's Spirit.
Rick Warren

SOMETHING TO THINK ABOUT

Worship reminds you of the awesome power of God. So worship Him daily, and allow Him to work through you every day of the week (not just on Sunday).

Devotion #94

THE CONTINUING SEARCH FOR WISDOM

Wisdom is the principal thing; therefore get wisdom.
And in all your getting, get understanding.
Proverbs 4:7 NKJV

Now that you've graduated, your head is undoubtedly filled with valuable information. But, there is much yet to learn. Wisdom is like a savings account: If you add to it consistently, then eventually you'll have a great sum. The secret to success is consistency.

Do you seek wisdom? Then keep learning. Seek wisdom every day, and seek it in the right place. That place, of course, is, first and foremost, the Word of God. When you study God's Word and live according to His commandments, you will surely become wise, and because of your wisdom, you will be blessed by your Father in heaven.

If you call upon the Lord and seek to see the world through His eyes, He will give you guidance and perspective. If you make God's priorities your priorities, He will lead you along a path of His choosing. If you study God's teachings, you will be reminded that God's reality is the ultimate reality.

As you accumulate wisdom, you may feel the need to share your insights with friends and family members. If so, remember this: your actions must reflect the values that you hold dear. The best way to share your wisdom—perhaps the only way—is not by your words, but by your example.

MORE FROM GOD'S WORD ABOUT WISDOM

The fear of the Lord is the beginning of wisdom; a good understanding have all those who do His commandments. His praise endures forever.
Psalm 111:10 NKJV

Therefore, everyone who hears these words of Mine and acts on them will be like a sensible man who built his house on the rock. The rain fell, the rivers rose, and the winds blew and pounded that house. Yet it didn't collapse, because its foundation was on the rock.
Matthew 7:24–25 HCSB

A wise man will hear and increase learning, and a man of understanding will attain wise counsel.
Proverbs 1:5 NKJV

Teach me, O Lord, the way of Your statutes, and I shall keep it to the end.
Psalm 119:33 NKJV

If we neglect the Bible, we cannot expect to benefit
from the wisdom and direction that result
from knowing God's Word.

Vonette Bright

Wisdom always waits for the right time to act,
while emotion always pushes for action right now.

Joyce Meyer

Knowledge is horizontal.
Wisdom is vertical; it comes down from above.

Billy Graham

Wise people listen to wise instruction, especially
instruction from the Word of God.

Warren Wiersbe

SOMETHING TO THINK ABOUT

Simply put, wisdom starts with God. If you don't have God's wisdom—and if you don't live according to God's rules—you'll pay a big price later.

Devotion #95

OVERCOMING PESSIMISM

Cast your burden on the Lord,
and He will support you;
He will never allow the righteous to be shaken.
Psalm 55:22 HCSB

Pessimism and Christianity don't mix. Why? Because Christians have every reason to be optimistic about life here on earth and life eternal. As C. H. Spurgeon observed, "Our hope in Christ for the future is the mainstream of our joy." But sometimes, we fall prey to worry, frustration, anxiety, or sheer exhaustion, and our hearts become heavy. What's needed is plenty of rest, a large dose of perspective, and God's healing touch, but not necessarily in that order.

Today, make this promise to yourself and keep it: vow to be a hope-filled Christian. Think optimistically about your life, your profession, and, of course, your future. Trust your hopes, not your fears. Take time to celebrate God's glorious creation. And then, when you've filled your heart with hope and gladness, share your optimism with others. They'll be better for it, and so will you. But not necessarily in that order.

Lord, I turn my hope to You. My God, I trust in You.
Psalm 25:1-2 HCSB

A pessimist is someone who believes that when her cup runneth over she'll need a mop.
Barbara Johnson

To lose heart is to lose everything.
John Eldredge

Never yield to gloomy anticipation.
Place your hope and confidence in God.
He has no record of failure.
Mrs. Charles E. Cowman

SOMETHING TO THINK ABOUT

Pessimism and Christianity don't mix. If you genuinely believe that God is good and that His Son died for your sins, how can you be pessimistic about your future? The answer, of course, is that you can't!

Devotion #96

SEEKING STRENGTH FROM GOD

The Lord is my strength and my song;
He has become my salvation.
Exodus 15:2 HCSB

Where do you go to find strength? The gym? The health food store? The espresso bar? There's a better source of strength, of course, and that source is God. He is a never-ending source of strength and courage if you call upon Him.

Have you "tapped in" to the power of God? Have you turned your life and your heart over to Him, or are you muddling along under your own power? The answer to this question will determine the quality of your life here on earth and the destiny of your life throughout all eternity. So start tapping in—and remember that when it comes to strength, God is the Ultimate Source.

He gives power to the weak,
and to those who have no might He increases strength.
Isaiah 40:29 NKJV

Measure the size of the obstacles against
the size of God.
Beth Moore

God walks with us. He scoops us up in His arms or
simply sits with us in silent strength
until we cannot avoid the awesome recognition
that yes, even now, He is here.
Gloria Gaither

God will never lead you where
His strength cannot keep you.
Barbara Johnson

SOMETHING TO THINK ABOUT

If your energy is low or your nerves are frazzled, perhaps you need to slow down and have a heart-to-heart talk with God. And while you're at it, remember that God is bigger than your problems . . . much bigger.

Devotion #97

CHOOSING THE POSITIVE PATH

But the path of the just is like the shining sun,
that shines ever brighter unto the perfect day.
The way of the wicked is like darkness;
they do not know what makes them stumble.
Proverbs 4:18-19 NKJV

When Jesus addressed His disciples, He warned that each one must, "take up his cross and follow Me." The disciples must have known exactly what the Master meant. In Jesus' day, prisoners were forced to carry their own crosses to the location where they would be put to death. Thus, Christ's message was clear: in order to follow Him, Christ's disciples must deny themselves and, instead, trust Him completely. Nothing has changed since then.

If we are to be dutiful disciples of the One from Galilee, we must trust Him and we must follow Him. Jesus never comes "next." He is always first. He shows us the path of life.

Do you seek to be a worthy disciple of Jesus? Then pick up His cross today and follow in His footsteps. When you do, you can walk with confidence: He will never lead you astray.

MORE FROM GOD'S WORD ABOUT FOLLOWING JESUS

But whoever keeps His word, truly in him the love of God is perfected. This is how we know we are in Him: the one who says he remains in Him should walk just as He walked.

1 John 2:5-6 HCSB

We encouraged, comforted, and implored each one of you to walk worthy of God, who calls you into His own kingdom and glory.

1 Thessalonians 2:12 HCSB

The one who loves his life will lose it, and the one who hates his life in this world will keep it for eternal life. If anyone serves Me, he must follow Me. Where I am, there My servant also will be. If anyone serves Me, the Father will honor him.

John 12:25-26 HCSB

You did not choose Me, but I chose you. I appointed you that you should go out and produce fruit, and that your fruit should remain, so that whatever you ask the Father in My name, He will give you.

John 15:16 HCSB

God's promises aren't celestial life preservers that
He throws out to strangers in the storm.
They are expressions of His love and care,
given to His children who walk with Him
and seek to obey Him.

Warren Wiersbe

You can't walk with God and hold hands
with Satan at the same time.

Anonymous

Be such a person, and live such a life,
that if every person were such as you,
and every life a life like yours,
this earth would be God's Paradise.

Phillips Brooks

SOMETHING TO THINK ABOUT

Following Christ is a matter of obedience. If you want to be a little more like Jesus . . . learn about His teachings, follow in His footsteps, and obey His commandments.